D1466143

CLUES

641.692 SAR ...B & ABALONE; WEST COA   LC CS

M 00 0140571 E

641.692
Sarvis, Shirley
  Crab & abalone, west coast ways
with fish & shellfish.

Date Due

SJ 70109	9/21/94	

CUMBERLAND COUNTY LIBRARY
BRIDGETON, N.J. 08302

PRINTED IN U.S.A.

CRAB & ABALONE

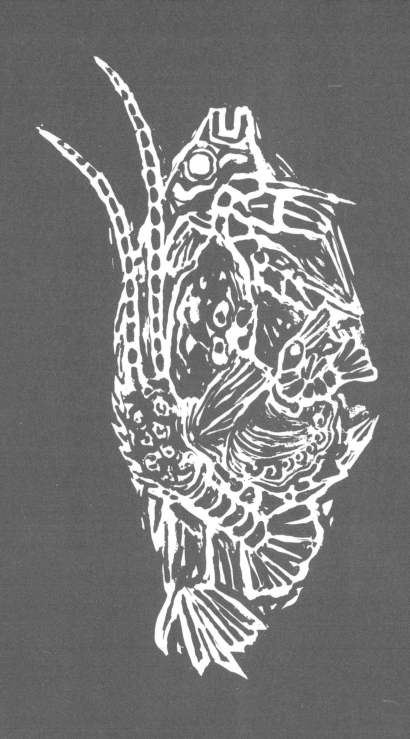

CRAB & ABALONE

WEST COAST WAYS WITH FISH & SHELLFISH

BY SHIRLEY SARVIS

DESIGNED & ILLUSTRATED BY TONY CALVELLO

THE BOBBS-MERRILL COMPANY Indianapolis New York

The Bobbs-Merrill Company, Inc.
A Subsidiary of Howard W. Sams & Co., Inc.,
Publishers • Indianapolis • Kansas City • New York

First printing, 1968

Copyright © 1968 by Shirley Sarvis and Tony Calvello

All rights reserved

Library of Congress catalog card number: 68-15810

Printed in the United States of America

From Shirley to Phyllis and family
From Tony to Sandy, Angela, Lynn, John and Tony

CONTENTS

Acknowledgments

It would not be possible to list all of the seafood-interested individuals who have so generously given their good ideas, time, and friendly advice toward the preparation of this book. Great thanks are due all of them; very special thanks go to these people and organizations:

Ralph Ferrandini—*U.S. Bureau of Commercial Fisheries, San Francisco*
Ross Hatton—*U.S. Bureau of Commercial Fisheries, Terminal Island, California*
Roy C. Stevens—*U.S. Bureau of Commercial Fisheries, Seattle*
Marine Resources Operations Laboratory, California Department of Fish and Game
Robert Thompson—*Public Relations, The Wine Institute, San Francisco*
Mrs. Robert Thompson—*San Francisco*
Annabel Post—*Palo Alto, California*
Edward W. Harvey—*Otter Trawl Commission, State of Oregon, Astoria*
Ken Sato—*Monterey, California*
T. J. Risoli—*U.S. Bureau of Commercial Fisheries, New York*
Ernie Cuneo—*San Francisco*

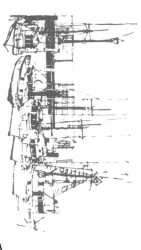

INTRODUCTION

In the winter, a San Franciscan walks the wooden walks of Fisherman's Wharf, reads again the names of the crammed-together fishing boats and wonders on the expanse of the day's crab catch. A foggy Pacific breeze chills him; he sniffs the wet salt air and knows that the taste he'd like most right now is an Italian fisherman's crab Cioppino—with some crusty San Francisco sourdough bread and a bottle of Napa Valley Barbera.

An old Sicilian fisherman plays bocce ball on the sands of the Monterey wharf. He thinks back to the big fishing days before the sardines disappeared, and recalls tales of Steinbeck's Cannery Row that top Steinbeck. When he thinks of fish-eating, he exults over the lowly fish and scorns the boneless fried fish that the restaurant customers seek. He remembers the best fish he ever tasted—barbecued anchovies, with a bottle of red wine and a loaf of Italian bread.

It is summer in Oregon, and the salmon run is on. The great king salmon swim out of the salt waters of the Pacific and up the fresh-water Columbia River to spawn. Now is when their flesh is richest, for they've laid down layers of protective fat for their noneating journey upstream. This is when Northwesterners prize them most of all and plot whole-salmon barbecues to inaugurate the salmon season. The old-timers plank and smoke-barbecue by an open fire, as the Northwest Indians taught their fathers to do. The younger cooks grill their salmon on a smoke-enclosing, hooded brazier.

On a morning in the mountain country of the Sierra, a lone camper wakes up in a damp sleeping bag, sees the sun glinting through the pines, smells the fresh morning air, and thinks of the breakfast before him: the morning's mountain trout catch, each fish wrapped in thin ham and sizzled over the campfire.

In the southern fishing ports, the commercial fishermen search the landing docks for the best eating for tonight's supper: A San Diego old-timer seeks the most refined sea bass, the totuava. The tenderloin of the totuava makes the richest, moistest eating of charcoal-broiled sea flesh. A fish wholesaler in Los Angeles chooses a local lobster, brilliantly vermilion, for a summertime salad of lobster meat chunks tossed with fresh oranges from the nearby citrus groves. . . .

They all know their seafood. The waters and the fruits of those waters are their environment. They all know what is best in their territory. They all yearn for the familiar goodness of their own region's best fish dish—as a Genoese longs for *pesto* or a Britisher for a pint of bitter.

Seafood is the source of some of the best eating in the West. Westerners who know good food know that, and live that way, and eat that way. Seafood is native, fresh, and a main part of the good-food, good-life surroundings.

But a Westerner's approach to fish and shellfish is unlike anyone else's. It is the way people eat—as much as the regional fishes, cooks and eaters—that sets West

Coast fish-eating apart from that of everywhere else. Westerners eat (and cook) in an unrule-bound way. And that lets them eat and cook with real flair and flexibility.

West Coast cooking is influenced by the cuisines of the whole world. Western cooks borrow from every nationality because they descend from every nationality. The West Coast ports call in ships, travelers, and food ideas from the whole world. The West may be a melting pot of many cuisines, but the result is a cuisine that is strictly their own. They borrow nuggets of wisdom from the old cuisines, but turn them into something that is of themselves.

There is an eagerness about the West that invites innovation. Westerners cook and eat creatively, just as they avidly experiment in other realms. But this exploration has as its goal supremely fine eating, not innovation for its own sake; and it is controlled by the sophistication of well taste-traveled Westerners. Western casualness gives a freedom to living and cooking that urges new experience.

The Western adjuncts to seafood are superb. There is almost an embarrassment of riches that sets Westerners in the midst of a near-paradise of fine foods and wines. This abundance of foodstuffs allows for unique linkages and exotic combinations of different foods.

So far as cookery is concerned, Western seafood is generally translatable to fish from other waters or frozen fish. The recipes in this book are written and tested so that these West Coast dishes can be accomplished with non-West Coast fishes that are similar. ("After all, fish is fish," declared one unfussy old-timer.) And anyone who faces facts has to concede that much of West Coast fish-eating today is no longer just of indigenous fish. The Western seafood appetite is too large; the local fish supplies are too small; imports arrive in fine eating condition; and cosmopolitan tastes sometimes call for something from far away.

This book cites the best Western ways with fish and shellfish.

This is not a definitive guide to the fish and shellfish dishes of the West Coast. It is not even necessarily a representative collection. It is certainly not a basic seafood cookbook. It is rather a selection of the stunning Western seafood dishes.

These are dramatic and wonderful fish dishes—often dramatic because they are wonderful. They tend to be simple recipes—because of the belief that fine seafood needs so little else to make it marvelous. Yet they are the flamboyant fish and shellfish dishes that typify the wide-handedness of the Western cooks who think (and cook) in stunning terms. This book is for lady *and* gentleman cooks.

This book is the result of searching up and down the Coast for the finest seafood eating and asking: What is the very best fish here? What is the best way to cook it? Who cooks it best? Where can we find that cook?

These recipes come from sources as close to the fish and fishing waters as possible—fishermen and their wives, fish vendors, a few restaurant chefs, and creative home cooks. This book is built on the premise that the people who know fish best cook it best. (Often those who know fish best are the commercial fishermen who make their livelihood by it. Fishermen and fishermen's wives cook wisely what they know well; they've worked with fish a lot, and that underwrites their confidence in experimenting further. The fishing folk love to eat fish because they know the glory of what they're catching, cooking and eating.) Every good fish cook has one cardinal rule: "Do not overcook fish!" You cook fish just to heat it through so the structure sets and firms, and that is all—never to tenderize it. It helps to think in terms of *minutes* of cooking fish, not parts of hours.

These are the kinds of recipes selected and groomed for this book:

1. The best versions of the traditional and regional fish and shellfish dishes
2. Recipes heretofore held in the memories of the superb seafood cooks
3. Current innovations in Western seafood cookery.

You will find only a few restaurant recipes, since this book is written for home cooks. The best home cooking originates in homes and the best restaurant cooking in restaurants. Home cooking most accurately reflects the essence of Western seafood tastes; cooks cook the way they like to eat.

The frank preponderance of crab recipes reflects the high esteem in which we hold our sweet-meated Dungeness crab.

There is a fair amount of wine talk. This is to help give you a guide to associating California wines with Western seafood so your pleasure in both is enhanced. To one who is food-knowledgeable, these wine suggestions may give a starting point for choosing the wine to go with a new dish. To one who is wine-knowledgeable, the description of the wine that goes with a dish will somewhat describe the dish; and certainly, sometimes, you'll want to plan a fish dish around an extraordinary wine. From time to time, there is a specific wine recommended at the end of a recipe, recalled from fond memory. These suggestions are not hard-bound rules; there is no intent to be precious about what goes with what. The wine approach of the book is the same as that of Westerners: They want the right wine, the complementing wine; but they also take it as the pleasant thing it is—not too formally or loaded with protocol.

This unorthodox cookbook chaptering reflects the unorthodox Western approach to seafood and the unexpected shape of the stories behind the way of Western seafood eating.

This book is meant to convey the flamboyance of Western fish, fishermen, fishing waters—and to exalt the West's exciting seafood eating.

CHAPTER 1
FRUITED FISH

Think of fish, and you almost automatically think of lemon. Think of fish and you don't automatically think of fruit, which, of course, lemon is. That lovely yellow citrus fruit has become so established as a near-essential for fish that we rarely even think of it as fruit.

But lemon, as a fruit, leads the way to all sorts of other fruits with fishes and to the conclusion that fruits of some nature are almost *de rigueur* for enhancing the flavor of fish. It actually turns out that most fish dishes depend upon fruit in some form for their verve.

It isn't always lemon. Fruits are used with fishes in many more ways. The Veronique treatment is an obvious one—with white grapes in a buttery sauce tumbling over delicately poached sole. Seafood curries contain apples and call on raisins and pineapple and fruit chutneys for condiment. Sole and bananas are a pairing in many parts of the world. Grapes, in the form of wine, appear endlessly in seafood saucing and poaching. Escoffier even writes of mackerel with green gooseberry sauce!

Pursue the fruits and fishes theme in the West, and you come up with such fascinating combinations as crab and litchi nuts under a macadamia-nut dressing, chilled fresh peach slices and ocean shrimp together for a first course, sole and papaya butter-broiled together. . . .

The list goes on. But the point is that fruit with fish leads to lovely and exotic eating, particularly in the West, where the fruits that fish can call upon stretch to pineapple, apricots, bananas, avocados, grapefruit, oranges, lemons, limes, and beyond.

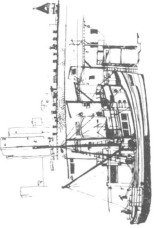

More than one visiting Easterner has been astounded to order a shrimp cocktail in the West and find tiny little curls of pink brought to him—instead of the big, peach-colored arcs of shellfish that he thought were shrimp. He has just discovered the tiny ocean shrimp that come from all along our coast, Alaska to Pismo Beach.

In Western terminology, shrimp versus prawn is a matter of size. A shrimp is a little thing, with body meat up to about one and a half inches long; any larger and it is unofficially a prawn. In the East, all sizes are called shrimp.

In the West, this first course would most likely be shrimp, but it could be prawns. In the East, you can do it with any size shrimp.

PERNOD PEACHES AND PRAWNS—FIRST COURSE

½ cup catsup
2 teaspoons Pernod
2 cups thin slices of fresh ripe peaches
½ pound tiny shrimp or ⅔ pound cooked, shelled, and deveined medium-size prawns
soft lettuce leaves

Combine catsup and Pernod and chill. Arrange peaches and shrimp in lettuce-lined stemmed seafood cocktail glasses or on small lettuce-lined plates; spoon catsup mixture over. Makes 4 to 6 servings.

WATERCRESS WINE SCALLOPS WITH GRAPEFRUIT

1½ pounds fresh scallops
1½ cups white table wine
2 large grapefruit, peeled and cut into
    sections, membrane removed
½ cup melted butter
salt
paprika
watercress, finely chopped and sprigs

Rinse and drain scallops. Put into a saucepan with wine; bring to a boil, then reduce heat, cover, and simmer for 8 minutes. Drain scallops and grapefruit sections in 4 to 6 well-buttered ¼-inch-thick slices. Arrange scallops and grapefruit sections in 4 to 6 well-buttered scallop shells or individual baking dishes or in a single shallow baking platter. Pour butter evenly over scallops and fruit. Sprinkle with salt and paprika. Bake in a moderate oven (350°) for 6 minutes or until heated through. Sprinkle generously with chopped watercress; garnish with watercress sprigs. Makes 4 main-dish or 6 first-course servings.

Wine suggestion: Paul Masson Emerald Dry

Serve with buttered toast and white wine as a first course. Or serve as a main course.

16

Sole and bananas are a combination known in many cuisines. But with papaya, too, it is West Coast.

Western flatfish are actually flounders, but they are commonly called sole. Western flounder experts rank Petrale the most delicate of them all.

PAPAYA GOLD SOLE

4 sole fillets, about 1½ pounds total
salt and pepper
3 ripe but firm bananas
lemon juice
1 large half-ripe papaya
½ cup butter
2 tablespoons fresh lemon juice
⅓ cup chopped fresh parsley

Wipe sole with a damp cloth and arrange in a single layer in a buttered broiling-serving platter. Sprinkle with salt and lightly with pepper to season. Peel bananas, cut into ½-inch-thick deep diagonal slices, and dip into lemon juice. Peel papaya, remove seeds, and cut into ½-inch-thick lengthwise slices. Arrange fruits alongside sole. Dot fish and fruit with ¼ cup of the butter. Broil about 3 inches from heat for about 5 minutes or just until fish flakes easily with a fork. Meantime, heat remaining butter until it foams and browns; stir in the 2 tablespoons lemon juice and parsley. Pour over broiled fish and fruit. Makes 4 servings.

Wine suggestion: Souverain Johannisberg Riesling

CUMIN-SMOKED SABLEFISH WITH PINEAPPLE

If your barbecue brazier does not have a hood for smoking, fashion one of heavy aluminum foil and fit it over grill. You want only a mild smoking here.

Pacific Ocean sablefish (also called black cod or butterfish) is ideal for this. Or use another large, white-fleshed, and moderately fat fish.

Cold ale is the thing to drink.

2 pounds sablefish fillet
salt
about 12 spears fresh pineapple sliced
½ inch thick
cumin butter (recipe below)

Form heavy aluminum foil into small trays the size of the fillets and about 1 inch deep. Cut a flat piece of foil just large enough to hold the pineapple arranged in a single layer. Wipe fish with a damp cloth, and sprinkle with salt. Place fish in trays and pineapple on foil on grill over low wood coals or coals of briquets sprinkled with soaked smoke chips. Brush fish and pineapple generously with cumin butter. Cover grill with hood or foil. Cook until fish loses translucency and flakes with a fork, about 20 minutes for ¾-inch-thick fillets. Lift hood, baste, and check for doneness about every 5 minutes. Cut fish into serving pieces, and serve pineapple alongside. Makes 4 servings.

Cumin butter: *Combine ½ cup melted butter, 3 tablespoons fresh lemon juice, and 1 teaspoon crushed cumin seeds.*

18

"A nice cool salad for summer. I like beer with it myself."

Carl Merry is a fish wholesaler in Los Angeles, and this salad is his invention. He says he discovered the triangular flavor linkage of fruit and shellfish and mayonnaise; mayonnaise does the blending. You can use grapefruit or pineapple instead of the orange, shrimp or crab instead of the lobster.

Mr. Merry uses meat of the local spiny lobster. You can use any cooked lobster meat.

Make the nutmeg rasping as generous as your taste dictates.

19

ORANGE AND LOBSTER SALAD

¾ pound cooked and chilled
   lobster meat
3 chilled oranges (preferably navel)
½ cup finely sliced celery
2 tablespoons chopped fresh parsley
1½ tablespoons finely sliced green
   onions with part of green tops
about ¼ cup mayonnaise
pinch of salt
salad greens
freshly grated nutmeg (or ground
   nutmeg)

Cut lobster meat into bite-size chunks. Peel oranges, cut into ½-inch-thick slices and quarter each slice. Gently toss lobster, oranges, celery, parsley, and onions with enough mayonnaise to moisten and salt to season. Arrange in a chilled shallow salad bowl or platter lined with salad greens. Grate nutmeg over the top. Makes 4 servings.

MUSCAT SOLE

The grapes must be Muscat; if you can't get them fresh, use the canned ones available in specialty food markets.

This is perhaps at its best in the autumn when the fresh Muscats are in. It makes a delightful morning fish dish to serve at brunch with a fruity, light wine.

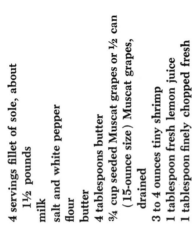

4 servings fillet of sole, about
1½ pounds
milk
salt and white pepper
flour
butter
4 tablespoons butter
¾ cup seeded Muscat grapes or ½ can
(15-ounce size) Muscat grapes,
drained
3 to 4 ounces tiny shrimp
1 tablespoon fresh lemon juice
1 tablespoon finely chopped fresh
parsley

Dip sole fillets in milk, season with salt and pepper, and coat lightly with flour. Heat until bubbly about ⅛ inch butter in frying pan. Sauté sole over medium-high heat until browned, about 1 minute on each side. Remove to warm serving platter or plates. Discard any excess butter in frying pan. Add the 4 tablespoons butter to the frying pan and heat until it foams and browns. Add grapes and shrimp and just heat through; pour over sole. Sprinkle with lemon juice and parsley. Makes 4 servings.

Wine suggestion: Paul Masson Rhine Castle

Hawaii has her influence on the Western mainland—here in a salad with tropical ingredients of macadamia nuts and litchi nuts.

CRAB AND MACADAMIA TROPICAL PLATTER

¾ pound fresh crab meat (mostly legs, if possible)
2 small grapefruit, peeled and cut into sections
1 large avocado, peeled and sliced
1 can (about 11 ounces) litchi nuts, drained
crisp lettuce leaves
about ¾ cup salted macadamia nuts, chopped
lemon dressing (recipe below)

Arrange crab, grapefruit, avocado slices, and litchi nuts on lettuce on 4 chilled plates. Sprinkle with macadamia nuts. Generously pour or spoon on dressing. Pass remaining dressing. Makes 4 luncheon-salad servings.

Lemon dressing: *Shake or beat together 1 cup salad oil, ¼ cup fresh lemon juice, 1 teaspoon grated lemon peel, about ½ teaspoon salt, ½ teaspoon dry mustard, and ¼ teaspoon coarsely ground black pepper.*

Wine suggestion: Paul Masson Emerald Dry

ARMENIAN STUFFED MUSSELS OR CLAMS (MIDIA DOLMA)

Many of the Armenians in the Far West are clustered in California's interior, the San Joaquin Valley, near Fresno. Still, they manage to get fresh mussels from the Coast (or clams when mussels are out of season) for their traditional stuffed-mussel appetizer or first course.

2 dozen large mussels or steaming clams

2 large onions, finely chopped

about 3 tablespoons olive oil

about ½ teaspoon salt

½ teaspoon *each* ground allspice and black pepper

½ cup uncooked long-grain white rice

3 tablespoons butter

4 tablespoons dried currants

4 tablespoons chopped fresh parsley

4 tablespoons pine nuts, lightly toasted

parsley sprigs and lemon wedges for garnish

Scrub mussels or clams well with a brush; soak in cold water for 1 hour, drain, and rinse. Place in a kettle with about ½ inch water in bottom; cover, bring to a boil, and cook for about 5 minutes or until shells pop open. Drain, saving liquid. Remove mussels from shells; save shells. In a frying pan or casserole with cover, sauté onions in the olive oil until limp. Stir in salt, allspice, pepper, and rice. Add 1¼ cups of the liquid reserved from cooking mussels (add water if necessary). Bring to a boil, then cover and simmer for 20 minutes or just until rice is tender. Heat butter until it foams and browns; add to cooked rice mixture, along with mussels, currants, chopped parsley, and pine nuts; toss gently to mix. Taste and add salt if necessary. Spoon rice mixture into mussel shells. Place on a baking-serving platter (or shallow pan) and bake in a moderate oven (350°) for a few minutes until heated through. Garnish with parsley sprigs and lemon wedges. Makes 6 to 8 first-course servings.

Wine suggestion: Wente Sauvignon Blanc

The fruit of the grape vine and the lemon tree:

For some unknown reason, the North Italians around San Francisco call anything "à la Bordelaise" if it's done in a sauce or seasonings of olive oil, garlic, and parsley, and sometimes white wine. They apply this marvelous à la Bordelaise freely, yet invariably successfully, to their seafood.

The young Piedmontese who cooks this calls her sauce "Bordelaise," but she's switched the olive oil to butter and the white wine to brandy.

Be sure to add the parsley and garlic just at the end—to keep the parsley bright and the garlic nonbitter.

ALDA'S SOLE À LA BRANDY BORDELAISE

4 servings fillet of sole (about 1½
  pounds total)
salt and pepper
2 eggs
salad oil (preferably peanut)
½ cup butter
2 tablespoons brandy
1½ tablespoons fresh lemon juice
⅓ cup chopped fresh parsley
1 clove garlic, minced or mashed

Wipe sole with a damp cloth; season on both sides with salt and pepper. Beat eggs with a fork just until blended. In a large frying pan, heat ⅛ inch salad oil over moderately high heat. Dip each fillet into egg, then place in frying pan. Sauté until golden on one side; turn carefully, and cook until fish flakes with a fork, about 3 to 5 minutes total. Remove to warm serving platter. (If necessary, keep warm in oven until all fish are cooked.) Heat butter until it foams and browns. Stir in all at once brandy, lemon juice, parsley, and garlic; pour over sole while bubbling. Serve immediately. Makes 4 servings.

APRICOT PRAWN SAUTÉ

A skillet supper for June or July from California's apricot-growing Santa Clara Valley. After the fresh-apricot season, use dried apricots.

Serve buttered hot steamed white rice alongside. Squeeze lime juice over prawns and rice as you eat.

6 tablespoons butter

2 cups fresh apricot halves (or 1 cup dried apricots, cooked until barely tender and drained well)

1½ pounds uncooked large prawns, shelled, deveined, and patted dry

about ¾ teaspoon salt

about ⅛ teaspoon freshly ground black pepper

¼ cup finely chopped mango chutney

2 tablespoons white wine vinegar

1 teaspoon ground ginger

½ teaspoon dry mustard

⅛ teaspoon ground cloves

¾ cup sliced green onions with part of green tops

finely chopped toasted almonds

lime wedges

Melt butter in a large frying pan over medium heat. Add apricots and prawns and turn just to coat with butter. Sprinkle with salt and pepper. Mix chutney, vinegar, ginger, mustard, and cloves, and add. Sauté, turning occasionally, just until prawns are pink and firm, about 8 minutes. Add onions, and just heat through. Sprinkle generously with almonds. Garnish with lime wedges. Makes 4 to 6 servings.

In the Far West, natural ingredients are sand dabs and California oranges. Elsewhere, use any small fish suitable for grilling whole with delicate flesh (such as rex sole, turbot, or trout—or use the sauce on sautéed sole fillets) and the oranges of your locality.

For these fish of delicate flesh and flavor, the mellow citrus of orange is more sweet and suitable than the usual lemon. And cream carries on the smoothness.

ORANGE SAND DABS UNDER BROWN-BUTTERED CREAM

4 cleaned whole sand dabs or other fish, about ½ pound each
½ cup butter
¼ cup dry white wine
½ cup heavy cream
3 tablespoons chopped fresh parsley
1 teaspoon grated fresh orange peel
freshly ground black pepper and salt
2 oranges, cut into wedges

Rinse fish and wipe dry. Melt about 1½ tablespoons of the butter and brush over fish. Place on a well-oiled grill and charcoal-grill over medium-low heat just until flesh loses translucency. (Or broil in oven: Place in buttered pan about 3 inches below heat for about 2½ minutes each side or until flesh is opaque.) Heat remaining butter until it foams and browns deeply. Add wine, and boil for a few moments, until it reduces slightly. Stir in cream, parsley, and orange peel; bring to a boil, then simmer until slightly reduced, about 4 minutes. Season with pepper and salt if necessary. Pour over grilled fish. Garnish with orange wedges; squeeze juice over as you eat. Makes 4 servings.

LIME CEVICHE

From their Mexican neighbors, West-erners learned to "cook" sweet sea scal-lops with lime juice, and to eat them with Margaritas. On their own, they learned that Ceviche goes as well with Martinis as with Margaritas. (Or spoon Ceviche into lettuce-lined sherbet glasses and serve as a first course, with buttered toast alongside.)

Fresh coriander is the distinction of Ceviche. Ask for it in Mexican and Spanish markets as cilantro, in Chinese markets as yuen sai or Chinese parsley, in Portuguese markets as coentro. If you can't find it, substitute parsley or a bit of oregano, and expect a less exotic effect.

1 pound fresh scallops
about ½ cup fresh lime (or lemon) juice
1 tablespoon salad oil
1 large ripe tomato, peeled, seeded, and chopped
2 tablespoons finely sliced green onions with part of green tops
2 tablespoons minced canned green chiles
2 tablespoons finely chopped fresh coriander
salt and freshly ground black pepper
lettuce leaves
avocado slices for garnish

Cut large scallops into bite-size chunks. Place scallops in a bowl, cover with lime juice, and chill for 4 hours. Drain off juice. Gently toss scallops with oil, tomatoes, onions, chiles, coriander, and salt and pepper to taste. Arrange on lettuce-lined chilled serving platter, and garnish with avocado slices. Serve as appetizers with cocktail picks. Makes appetizers for about 8 (or first course for 6).

Those who scorn fish steaks in favor of fillets do it on the theory that steaking cuts the fibers short, leaving myriads of them stubbed on both surfaces; filleting leaves those tissue fibers smooth and undisturbed. To quote one: "No fish should be steaked. It's the worst thing you can do to fish. The fish flesh runs one way; if you cut it short, it draws up when it cooks. You end up with a bunch of straw in your mouth."

This dish is a testimony to the favor of the fillet, but actually halibut and sturgeon steaks bake very well this way, and so do salmon fillets and steaks.

The fruit is lemon.

HALIBUT IN LEMON CREAM

2 pounds halibut fillet, cut into serving-size pieces
salt
1 cup heavy (whipping) cream
1 tablespoon grated onion
1 teaspoon grated lemon peel
4 teaspoons fresh lemon juice
freshly ground black pepper (optional)
thin lemon slices for garnish

Wipe fish with a damp cloth; sprinkle lightly with salt. Arrange in a single layer in a shallow buttered baking dish. Combine cream, onion, lemon peel, lemon juice, and ½ teaspoon salt, and pour over fish. Bake, uncovered, in a hot oven (400°) for 20 minutes or until fish flakes with a fork. Spoon cream sauce over it as you serve. Grind on black pepper. Garnish with lemon slices. Makes 4 servings.

Wine suggestion: Beaulieu Vineyard Chablis

CONDIMENT TUNA CURRY SALAD

Condiments are a part of the salad curry rather than outside it. Good to serve for a buffet salad luncheon, with buttered hot French bread.

Use chunks of poached fresh tuna or quality canned tuna. You can do the same salad with chicken instead of tuna.

¾ cup mayonnaise
about 1 teaspoon curry powder (optional)
½ cup plumped seedless raisins
½ cup salted peanuts
½ cup finely slivered or chopped mango chutney (about one 8-ounce jar)
½ cup flaked coconut
2 cups bite-size chunks of poached tuna or 2 cans (about 7 ounces each) white or light, solid-pack or chunk tuna, drained
3 bananas
lettuce leaves
1 avocado, peeled and sliced
fresh lemon juice

Mix together the mayonnaise, curry, raisins, peanuts, chutney, and coconut. Toss gently with tuna. Cut half the bananas into crosswise slices, add to tuna, and toss gently. Arrange salad on lettuce-lined chilled platter. Cut remaining banana into long diagonal slices. Dip banana and avocado slices into lemon juice, and arrange as salad garnish. Makes 4 generous servings.

Note: To plump raisins, cover with hot water, let stand for 5 minutes, drain well.

28

CHAPTER 2

FISH FOR BREAKFAST

Westerners like seafood for breakfast for several reasons. It is not hackneyed. It is tasty and interesting enough to call for attentive eating. It is delicate enough to be suited to our relatively gentle tasting wishes in the morning. Smoked seafoods make a familiar extension of the smoked meats we all deem traditional for breakfast. Seafood makes breakfast important enough for leisurely eating and thus an accompanying wine.

We arrange it so that breakfast can sometimes be a time of dalliance.

Certainly seafood for breakfast is not exclusively Western. But some of the dishes are.

Many of these breakfast dishes might also be for brunch, or lunch, or dinner.

SOLE FILBERTINE

In the Oregon filbert country, they do the classic almondine treatment with filberts. On a late-summer morning, have sliced fresh peaches alongside.

4 servings

fillet of sole, about 1½ pounds
salt and pepper
butter
6 tablespoons butter
½ cup chopped filberts
3 tablespoons fresh lemon juice
¼ teaspoon salt
⅛ teaspoon ground nutmeg (optional)
dash of pepper
chopped fresh parsley

Season sole with salt and pepper. Heat until bubbly about ⅛ inch butter in frying pan. Sauté sole over medium-high heat until browned, about 1 minute on each side. Remove to warm serving platter or plates. Add the 6 tablespoons butter and filberts to frying pan and heat, stirring, until butter foams and browns lightly. Stir in lemon juice, salt, nutmeg, and pepper. Pour over sole. Sprinkle with parsley. Makes 4 servings.

Many people along the Pacific salmon coast kipper or smoke their own salmon. They might broil a piece of kippered salmon for breakfast (brush with butter, sprinkle with pepper, broil until brown) and serve it with this rich egg sauce.

Those with less abundance of salmon can have flakes of it in egg sauce, over crisp-toasted cornbread. Kippered salmon is better suited for this dish than is smoked salmon. But you can use smoked or even drained canned salmon; salt accordingly.

KIPPERED SALMON IN EGG SAUCE—CORNBREAD TOAST

2 tablespoons butter
1½ tablespoons flour
about ½ teaspoon salt
about ¼ teaspoon freshly ground
    black pepper
1½ cups milk
3 hard-cooked eggs
4 ounces kippered salmon, coarsely
    flaked
chopped fresh parsley
cornbread triangle slices, buttered and
    broil-toasted

In a saucepan, melt butter and stir in flour, salt, and pepper to make a smooth paste. Gradually add milk, cooking and stirring over medium heat to make a smooth sauce. Sieve one egg yolk. Chop or coarsely grate remaining eggs and white and add to sauce along with salmon; heat through. Serve over cornbread points. Sprinkle with sieved egg yolk and parsley. Makes 3 servings.

31

Breakfast bread should be toasted corn-bread or French bread with tomato preserves or honey.

GRILLED PROSCIUTTO TROUT

4 whole trout, each about ½ pound,
    cleaned
4 ounces thinly sliced Italian pros-
    ciutto or ham
salad oil
1 large banana, diagonally sliced
1 small avocado, peeled and sliced
    lengthwise
1 large orange, peeled and sliced
¾ cup butter
3 tablespoons fresh lemon juice
3 tablespoons snipped chives

Spiral-wrap each trout in prosciutto. Brush with salad oil. Place on well-greased grill and charcoal-grill over medium-low heat just until fish loses translucency. Arrange trout on warm serving platter or plates, and garnish with banana, avocado, and orange slices. Heat butter until it bubbles and turns golden brown. Stir in lemon juice and chives; pour over trout. Makes 4 servings.

Note: To cook trout in frying pan instead of grilling: Rinse each trout, dust with flour to coat, and spiral-wrap in prosciutto. Fry quickly in equal parts salad oil and butter about ¼ inch deep in frying pan. Top with chive butter as above.

Wine suggestion: Stony Hill Traminer

The sausage should not be a stuffing, just a seasoning—delicate enough so you can taste both it and the sole.

DR. PELLEGRINI'S SAUSAGE SOLE

¼ pound lean bulk pork sausage
2 tablespoons finely minced shallots
4 tablespoons finely chopped parsley
3 tablespoons tomato sauce
1 tablespoon fresh lemon juice
4 fillets of sole, about 1½ pounds
    total
salt and pepper
flour
butter
salad oil
4 tablespoons dry white table wine or
    dry vermouth

In a small frying pan, cook sausage over low heat until crumbly and well browned; pour off all drippings. Add shallots and 3 tablespoons of the parsley, and sauté just until limp. Stir in tomato sauce and lemon juice. Season sole fillets with salt and pepper, and coat one side of each fillet lightly with flour. Spread part of sausage mixture over half of unfloured side of each fillet. Fold each fillet in half, crosswise, and fasten at the end with a toothpick. Heat equal parts butter and salad oil about ⅛ inch deep in a frying pan. Place sole in pan, and cook over medium heat until lightly browned on both sides and fish flakes easily with a fork, about 8 minutes total. Sprinkle wine over sole, remove to warm serving plate, and sprinkle with remaining parsley. Makes 4 servings.

Hangtown Fry is one of the most renowned dishes of the West and it is strictly Western. The dish dates back to Gold Rush days. Many tales are told of its origin. One of the favorites is that when the sheriff of Hangtown (now Placerville, California) asked a condemned miner what he wanted for his last meal on earth, the man requested the three most expensive things in the world (that forty-niner world)—oysters, eggs, and bacon. The result was Hangtown Fry.

Nowadays, it is mostly made with Pacific oysters breaded, fried, folded into scrambled eggs, and topped with bacon strips. But Al Puccini (third generation, Italian commercial fish family, San Francisco–Oakland) has his special version—Hangtown Fry made with those exquisite, delicate, and costly little Olympia oysters. He has a whole jar of them (about eighty) cracker-crumbed and fried crisp, tucked into a three-egg omelet, and flanked by four strips of bacon. His may not be the typical Hangtown Fry, but it is a supreme one, and it probably vies with the original for its dearness.

This is Hangtown Fry in a more colorful way. For breakfast, it is sufficient as it is; for brunch, add French fried potatoes and a tossed green salad.

ELABORATED HANGTOWN FRY

¼ cup butter
½ cup finely diced green bell pepper
½ cup sliced green onions with part of green tops
1 jar (10 to 12 ounces) Pacific (or other) oysters, drained
8 to 12 slices bacon

8 eggs
½ cup milk
about 1 teaspoon salt
about ¾ teaspoon coarse black pepper
fine strips canned red pimento
finely chopped fresh parsley

Melt butter in a frying pan, add peppers and onions, and stir just to coat with butter. Add oysters (cut large Pacific oysters in half) and cook over low heat just until edges begin to curl, about 5 minutes; turn once. Meantime, in a separate large frying-serving pan, cook bacon until crisp; set aside. Pour off all but 3 tablespoons of the bacon drippings in frying pan. Beat eggs with milk, salt, and pepper; add to bacon drippings in pan, and scramble just until set. With slotted spoon, lift oysters and vegetables from pan and arrange over eggs. Garnish with pimentos and sprinkle with parsley. Serve immediately with bacon alongside. Makes 4 servings.

Bake individual platters of this Parmesan-crusted sole, asparagus, and eggs; or bake all on one large serving platter. Pass the pepper grinder.

BREAKFAST SOLE AND EGGS PARMESAN

½ cup soft butter
1 cup grated Parmesan cheese
4 small sole fillets (about ¼ pound *each*)
12 spears fresh asparagus, cooked just until tender and drained
4 eggs
chopped fresh parsley

Spread half the butter thickly over bottom of large baking-serving platter or 4 individual platters. Sprinkle evenly with half the Parmesan. Arrange sole in a single layer over cheese; dot with remaining butter; sprinkle with remaining Parmesan. Bake in a hot oven (400°) for 10 minutes, basting frequently with melted butter and cheese. Remove from oven, and arrange asparagus as a border garnish. Break eggs alongside sole. Spoon Parmesan drippings over eggs and asparagus. Return to oven, and bake for 5 minutes more or just until eggs are set. Sprinkle with parsley and serve immediately, spooning drippings over. Makes 4 servings.

BACON-BROILED LOBSTER

4 spiny lobster tails (about 8 ounces
  each) or 8 tails (about 4 ounces
  each)
3 slices bacon, cut into small pieces
4 tablespoons butter
1 fresh tomato, peeled, seeded, and
  finely chopped (or 4 tablespoons
  tomato sauce)
2 tablespoons minced chives
about ⅜ teaspoon salt
about ¼ teaspoon freshly ground
  black pepper
½ cup melted butter
2 tablespoons fresh lemon juice

Thaw frozen lobster tails. Cut away and remove under shells. Cut each large tail in half lengthwise through shell and lay flat, shell side down, on broiler pan; leave small tails whole and bend shells back, cracking some joints to prevent curling. Loosen lobster meat from shell and score meat about every half inch, cutting almost to shell. Cook bacon slowly until nearly crisp; pour off drippings. Add to bacon the 4 tablespoons butter, tomato, chives, salt, and pepper; spoon mixture over lobster meat and well into grooves. Broil about 5 inches from heat for about 7 minutes. Combine the ½ cup melted butter and lemon juice, and serve as a dip with lobster tails. Makes 4 servings.

Wine suggestion: Charles Krug Chardonnay

Fresh orange juice sprinkled with nutmeg, toasted English muffins, and lobster make a breakfast.

The shad in the springtime markets of the West comes from the Northwest rivers. Any shad from California must be caught by a sport fisherman but the stripped-out roe can be sold commercially.

Mrs. Scafine sells fine fish and shellfish in her family's market on Polk Street in San Francisco. And she knows well how to cook every one of the things she sells. You'd think she couldn't learn another thing about fish and fish cookery, but one day a fellow came in to buy shad roe and told her to try this; she did, thinks it's grand, and now recommends it:

The idea is simply olive oil for broiling-basting and flavor instead of the usual butter or bacon drippings. It lets you taste the roe more.

WESTERN SHAD ROE

1 large set shad roe (about ¾ pound)
olive oil
salt
crisp bacon strips
lemon wedges (optional)

Gently rinse roe and wipe dry. Sprinkle generously on both sides with salt to season. Place on well-oiled broiler pan. Broil about 4 inches from heat for about 5 minutes on each side or just until eggs are opaque white throughout (slit to center with small knife to test), brushing occasionally with more olive oil. Separate the set. Serve with bacon. Garnish with lemon. Makes 2 servings.

MADEIRA SHAD ROE

1 large set shad roe (about ¾ pound)
salt
about 6 tablespoons butter
3 to 4 ounces fresh mushrooms, thinly
  sliced
4 tablespoons dry to medium Madeira
watercress sprigs

Gently rinse roe and wipe dry. Sprinkle generously on both sides with salt to season. Melt 4 tablespoons of the butter in frying pan, add mushrooms, and sauté over medium heat until coated with butter and barely tender; push to side of pan. Add 2 tablespoons more butter, then the roe; sauté until browned on both sides and eggs are opaque throughout (slit to center with small knife to test), about 12 minutes total. Remove roe to warm serving platter. Add Madeira to frying pan, and cook and stir with mushrooms until slightly reduced. Pour sauce over roe. Garnish with watercress. Makes 2 servings.

Flame if you wish: As soon as Madeira warms in frying pan, light it; pour flaming sauce over roe.

A colorful cream and cheese whip melts into pan-browned sole fillets. Little ginger muffins are good with this.

MACADAMIA SOLE WITH PIMENTO CHEESE CREAM

4 servings fillet of sole, about 1½
  pounds
salt and pepper
flour
butter
pimento cheese cream (recipe below)
⅓ to ½ cup salted macadamia nuts,
  chopped

Season sole with salt and pepper; coat lightly with flour. Heat until bubbly about ⅛ inch butter in frying pan. Sauté sole over medium-high heat until browned, about 1 minute on each side. Remove to warm serving platter or plates. Spoon pimento cheese cream on top of fish; sprinkle with macadamia nuts. Makes 4 servings.

Pimento cheese cream: Beat 1 small package (3 ounces) softened cream cheese with 1 teaspoon fresh lemon juice and about ⅛ teaspoon each salt and pepper until creamy; fold into ½ cup heavy cream, softly whipped, along with 1 small can or jar (2 ounces) sliced pimentos, drained, and 3 tablespoons minced green onions with part of green tops.

SALMON AND RELISH EGGS

This is a Trader Vic creation—not done for his restaurants, but simply upon presentation of some smoked Columbia River salmon. He admits that canned or kippered salmon works almost as well; adjust salting.

If you can wait until lunch or brunch for this dish, have it with beer and rye bread. At breakfast, serve it with rye bread toast. Offer additional relish.

⅓ cup sliced green onions with part of green tops
4 tablespoons butter
2 tablespoons well-drained green-tomato relish
2 ounces smoked salmon, cut into pieces
4 eggs
4 tablespoons milk
about ½ teaspoon salt
about ⅛ teaspoon freshly ground black pepper

In a small pan, sauté onions in 2 tablespoons of the butter until limp. Remove from heat, add pickle relish and salmon, and turn just to mix. Meantime, melt remaining 2 tablespoons butter over medium-low heat in a separate frying pan. Beat eggs with milk, salt, and pepper; add to butter, and scramble just until set. Gently fold in salmon mixture, and serve immediately. Makes 2 servings.

You can sit in the Moby Dick Coffee Shop on Stearns Wharf, out over the Pacific fishing waters of Santa Barbara, and order a breakfast omelet of shrimp and crab meat. It comes all fatty filled and overflowing with shellfish. Or you can know a local fisherman or seafood lover, and he'll probably make one for you. Or you can make it yourself.

Season with ever the slightest bit of dill. (Use snipped fresh dill instead of dried if you have it.) Garnish with cucumber slices. Serve with rye toast and apple or currant jelly.

SHRIMP AND CRAB OMELET

1 tablespoon butter
about ⅛ teaspoon dill weed
2 ounces crab meat
1 ounce tiny shrimp
2 eggs
2 teaspoons water
about ⅛ teaspoon salt
dash of freshly ground black pepper
2 teaspoons butter
sliced fresh cucumbers

In a small frying pan, melt the tablespoon of butter with the dill; add crab and shrimp, and sauté just to coat with butter and heat through. Meantime beat eggs, water, salt, and pepper together with a fork. Heat the 2 teaspoons butter in a 7- to 9-inch omelet pan until it bubbles. Pour in egg mixture, and tilt pan so egg covers bottom. Lift egg edges with a thin-bladed spatula and tilt pan so uncooked egg flows to bottom of pan. When top is still creamy but barely set, spoon crab mixture down center. Fold top third of omelet over filling, and slip omelet out of pan onto warm serving plate, rolling pan so that folded section falls over its extended edge. Sprinkle very lightly with dill. Makes 1 serving.

SEATTLE FISH PUDDING WITH SLICK SAUCE

6 tablespoons butter
½ cup plus 2 tablespoons flour
2 cups milk
flaked dried cod (directions below)
6 eggs, separated

about 1 teaspoon ground nutmeg
about ½ teaspoon sugar
salt and pepper to taste
fine dry bread crumbs
slick sauce (recipe below)

Melt butter in a heavy saucepan. Stir in flour to make a smooth paste. Gradually add milk, and cook and stir over medium heat to make a smooth, thick sauce. Stir in flaked cod. Beat egg yolks and add to sauce, along with nutmeg, sugar, salt, and pepper. Beat egg whites until stiff but not dry. Gently and thoroughly fold half the whites into sauce; fold in remaining whites. Turn into a 2-quart soufflé dish which has been buttered and coated with crumbs. Bake in a moderate oven (375°) for 40 minutes. Serve immediately with slick sauce. Makes 6 to 8 servings.

Flaked cod: Soak ½ pound skinned and boned dried cod (or slightly more un-boned cod) in cold water for 24 hours, until it is very moist throughout; change water two or three times. (Or freshen cod according to package directions.) Simmer cod, covered, in water just to cover for 15 minutes or until tender; drain; remove skin and bones if necessary; flake finely.

Slick sauce: Beat together with electric beater until fluffy 1 cup each salted butter and sweet butter, softened. Gradually beat in fresh lemon juice to taste (about 2 tablespoons). Turn into serving bowl and sprinkle with ground nutmeg.

Of Danish descent, this dish is far more sumptuous than its title.

CHAPTER 3
THE CRAB INSTITUTION

DUNGENESS CRAB

Ecstasy over seafood seems largely a local matter. Southern Californians claim the ultimate in spiny lobsters with their Pacific Ocean catch, but a traveler from Portugal will declare his *lagosta* has better flavor. There's nothing like the bluepoints, say Easterners of oysters; and a Northwesterner will defy that with a devastating description of the rare little Olympias. Those who say the Dover sole is best would wage culinary war with a Petrale sole devotée.

The objective observer assumes these passions to be the products of tastes trained by living in a locale.

But when Westerners extol their local Dungeness crab, outsiders join in their jubilation over a crustacean so succulent. The Pacific Coast crab has become an institution. The Dungeness crab is to the West Coast what Maine lobster is to the East Coast—the unique offering from the sea, revered by natives and visitors alike.

At the opening of each season, a Roman Catholic priest blesses the crab fleet before it bobs out of San Francisco Bay. It is a blessing echoed and amened by crab *aficionados* everywhere of every faith—if their only faith is a reverence for the beautiful taste of crab.

The West Coast crab is the Dungeness crab (originally called Dungeness after a small town in Washington), sometimes also called market crab, Pacific crab, or white crab. It is found in waters from Monterey Bay to Alaska. Dungeness crabs range in size from one and one-half to three and one-half pounds, with two pounds about average. Their meat is in their eight legs, two claws, and body. Three to four pounds of whole crab yield about one pound (two cups, firmly packed) of meat. When buying cracked crab for main-course serving you count on approximately one large crab for two people or one small crab per person. The commercial catching season varies, but it usually runs from December through May.

The starting point for all eating is cracked crab. In season you buy whole crabs, freshly cooked in great boiling pots, from crab stands and fish vendors in fishing towns up and down the Coast. You choose your crabs, and the fish man will crack and clean them for you; and you take them home to pluck the white meat out of the leg and body shells with a crab pick or the point of a crab claw. You can buy live crabs and cook and crack them yourself, or have the crab vendor crack and clean live crabs before you cook them at home. To cook a whole crab: Pick up crab with kitchen tongs (or "Grab a crab by back two legs and he can't hurt you") and drop into a big kettle of boiling well-salted water. Cover, return water to boiling, and boil for 20 minutes—no more! Remove crab and plunge into cold water or cool on a rack. Cook cracked crab the same as whole, except boil for only 8 minutes.

A note on *crab butter:* This is the yellow-white, creamy fat that clings to the inside of the back shell (when raw, the crab butter is mustard-colored edged with brick red). It is much prized by those in the know for its natural essence-of-crab seasoning. When you buy cracked crab ask the vendor to save the butter for you. It is easiest to handle if you just take along the whole back, with the butter clinging inside.

Come early December and a San Franciscan's taster tells him it's time to start taking advantage of the season's glorious tasting of fresh Dungeness crab. The same thing happens in Monterey, Seattle, and everywhere along the Western crab coast. When the crab season first opens all a crab fan wants is cracked crab—the pure, unadulterated sweet meat. Sometime later in the season the sauces and crab dishes come into their own.

Obviously, nothing can compare with the splendor of a plump crab just pulled in, boiled before you, cracked, and eaten while it is still warm. But Dungeness crab is also a joy if you buy it freshly cooked and chilled. It even retains its delicate taste, though on a slightly lesser level, when frozen for out-of-season eating and for shipping to other parts of the nation.

For the following recipes that call for crab meat, you can use Alaska King crab or blue crab or any other crab meat you have. But bear in mind that they are at their best when executed with the Dungeness.

CRACKED CRAB IN SHELL

"Cracked crab" isn't one thing; it is several, depending upon your convictions. It is hot crab right out of the boiler pot. It is cold crab piled high and eaten with beer and mayonnaise and lemon and French bread. It is crab steamed just to rareness and savored warm, with a lot of cold dry white California Gewürz Traminer or Johannisberg Riesling. It is crab meat plucked from the shell and dipped into hot sherry butter as Easterners serve drawn butter with lobster. . . .

Dipping dressings for cracked crab are legion. Mayonnaise is classic for cold crab with beer—and most popular. Thereafter, there are many others, each highly recommended by its devotée.

The following are some convictions as to the best way to prepare cracked crab. Sources range from the outspoken purist to the believers in quite a few accompanying seasonings.

HOT CRAB OUT OF THE POT

"The best crab is right out of the boiler pot, so hot you can't hold it." "That's when it's got flavor. Once it cools down, the flavor's gone." "Accompaniment to cracked crab? If I want to eat crab, I want crab. If I want mayonnaise, I'll get a bologna sandwich and have mayonnaise."

COLD CRACKED CRAB AND BEER AND FRENCH BREAD

"Beer goes with crab, especially with mayonnaise." "Cracked crab and mayonnaise must have beer."

The best crab for cracked crab is the live crab you cook yourself. Wide tradition is to boil crab, but steaming crab produces perhaps the sweetest, juiciest flesh of all.

You can steam crab easily at home. All you need is a large kettle; the crab shell serves as its own steaming rack.

SIMPLY STEAMED CRAB FOR CRACKED CRAB

2 large live Dungeness crabs (about 6 pounds total), cleaned and cracked

Scrub crab pieces well with a brush. Cover bottom of a large kettle with about ½ inch of well-salted water. Bring to a boil. Add crab pieces, cover, and simmer for 9 minutes. Remove crab immediately and cool on a rack. Makes about 4 servings.

This dressing came from one of those crab-knowledgeable Eurekans who value the crab butter. The youngsters in the inventor's family invented their own style for eating: They use the dressing as a spread on French bread or as a crab dressing or as both. Their idea works well when you're serving cracked crab as a snack, with beer.

Locals give credit for the invention of their fresh-tasting namesake dressing to a little old lady who ran a "little old shack of a crab stand" in Eureka about twenty years ago.

LEMON CRAB BUTTER

crab butter from 2 cooked Dungeness
    crabs (about ½ cup)
4 to 6 tablespoons olive oil
3 tablespoons fresh lemon juice
2 drops liquid hot-pepper seasoning
about ¼ teaspoon freshly ground
    black pepper
salt

Mash crab butter with a fork. Beat in olive oil, lemon juice, liquid hot-pepper seasoning, pepper, and salt to taste. Makes dressing for 2 cracked crabs.

HUMBOLDT DRESSING

crab butter from 2 cooked Dungeness
    crabs (about ½ cup)
½ cup mayonnaise
1 teaspoon Worcestershire sauce
4 drops liquid hot-pepper seasoning
1 cup finely chopped celery
½ cup finely chopped fresh parsley
2 tablespoons thinly sliced green
    onions with part of green tops

Mash crab butter with a fork. Stir in mayonnaise, Worcestershire, liquid hot-pepper seasoning, celery, parsley, and onions. Cover and chill for 30 minutes before serving. Makes dressing for 2 cracked crabs.

This is a scheme for dipping chunks of crab meat, plucked from the shell, into a hot butter sauce in the same manner as Easterners handle their boiled lobsters. This slightly deviled sherry butter is superb when you're having cracked crab as an appetizer course and sipping dry sherry. (Or make butter-dipped crab into a meal with white wine and French bread; then use just melted butter, not sherry butter.)

For the ultimate here, you should steam or boil a cleaned and cracked live crab yourself and serve it while the meat is still hot. It is also excellent with cracked crab that has been commercially cooked and cooled; the hot butter will still warm the crab flesh enough to bring up its full nutty flavor.

DEVILED SHERRY BUTTER

½ cup (¼ pound) butter
2 teaspoons dry sherry
2 drops liquid hot-pepper seasoning

Melt butter; stir in sherry and liquid hot-pepper seasoning, and just heat through. Pour into individual cups or candle-warmed serving pots. Makes sauce for about 2 cracked crabs or about 4 to 6 first-course servings.

"Once you've had cracked crab marinated, you'll never like it any other way." So pronounced the two salty Italians who touted this recipe. "Do it this way. Then you really have a dish—if you like garlic. A nice glass of wine and toasted French bread are terrific with it. The more you eat the more you want. Now be plenty generous with the garlic."

JOE'S MARINATED CRACKED CRAB

2 large Dungeness crabs
(about 6 pounds total), cooked,
cleaned, and cracked
1 cup olive oil
⅓ cup red wine vinegar
3 large cloves garlic,
minced or mashed
about ¾ teaspoon salt
about ¼ teaspoon freshly ground
black pepper
½ cup chopped fresh parsley

Place crab in a deep bowl. Shake or beat together oil, vinegar, garlic, salt, pepper, and parsley. Pour over crab and let stand in a cool place for about 1½ hours; turn crab occasionally. To serve, heap crab on a platter; pour excess marinating sauce into individual bowls and serve as a dipping sauce. Makes about 4 servings.

Ever since Italians have been fishing crabs off San Francisco Bay and cooking them on their boats with garlic and tomato seasonings, they've been calling the resulting stew "cioppino." By now, it seems that for every fisherman, there's been a particular cioppino invention, so numerous are the claimed authentic versions.

Cioppino can be as simple as crab, garlic, and tomatoes, or complex enough to include prawns and clams and white-fleshed fish; onions, parsley, carrots, green peppers, or hot peppers; red wine or white wine; lemon juice or vinegar; basil, thyme, marjoram, oregano; cloves or cinnamon; sugar.

For some versions, the cioppino sauce should be almost as thin as a soup so it will take to lots of dunkings of crusty Italian bread. For others, it should be thick yet ample enough to sauce coils of hot spaghetti alongside. For still others, it should be extra spicy and thin so it will soak into garlic-buttered, toasted Italian bread lining the serving plates. Everyone considers an all-crab cioppino most luxurious.

The cioppino here is a purist's; smoothness is its nature. It calls for crab alone with its own natural crab-butter seasoning, garlic, tomatoes, salt, and pepper. To the mind of Mr. Hogan, the more you put with crab, the less you can taste the crab. He's been all over the world, sometimes rich, sometimes with pants and boots rotting; he's been catching and cooking fish since 1907; he's fished and sold fish at the end of San Francisco Fisherman's Wharf for thirty-five years; he believes in plain cooking so you get the "soul" of the fish flavor; his chubby admiring daughters boast that he's as grand a dancer as he is a fisherman and fish cook; nowadays, when he's not cooking a crab cioppino or onion spaghetti or helping his daughters wait on the fish-market customers, he's probably outwitting fellow poker players at a corner table of his Sausalito Cafe back of his open fish market. He's one of the best-loved old-timers on the wharf. He's a quiet, soft-spoken gentleman. His name is Antonio Tedesco; he's known only as Hogan.

He cooks a crab cioppino for his customers (all friends) whenever they wander in and ask for it, during the season.

His secret is (1) the crab-butter seasoning, "The best part of the crab," and (2) not overcooking any part of the dish— the sauce or the crab. To him, there's no sense in the theory of long hours of cooking the tomato sauce for the cioppino. Nor is there any sense in many seasonings—wine, herbs, "perfumes"; "garlic and onion are all you need." In twenty-five minutes from start to finish, he produces his cioppino.

Serve it with hot spaghetti alongside, cooked al dente ("It should be a little tough") and sprinkled with grated Parmesan and a grinding of black pepper. Also serve red wine and Italian bread.

HOGAN'S ALL-CRAB CIOPPINO

3 medium-sized Dungeness
  crabs (about 7 to 8 pounds total),
  cleaned and cracked
2 large onions, finely chopped
½ cup olive oil
3 large cloves garlic, minced or
  mashed
2 cans (8 ounces *each*) tomato sauce
crab butter from 3 crabs
about 1 teaspoon salt
about ½ teaspoon freshly ground
  black pepper
hot cooked spaghetti sprinkled with
  Parmesan and freshly ground
  black pepper
chopped fresh parsley

Scrub crab well. In a very large kettle, sauté onions in olive oil until golden. Stir in garlic, then tomato sauce, crab butter, salt, and pepper. Simmer for 5 minutes, stirring occasionally. Add crab, and simmer for 10 minutes. Taste sauce and correct seasoning. Serve onto heated shallow platters with spaghetti alongside, spooning sauce over crab and spaghetti. Sprinkle with parsley. Makes 4 to 6 servings.

Wine suggestion: A California Barbera

CRAB-BUTTERED CRAB

This is exotic. Simplicity makes it so.

If you want to serve this hot crab on a sauce-absorbing base, make a receptive toast base this way: Trim crusts from thin-sliced firm white bread, cut into triangles, and spread generously with a mixture of soft butter and a lot of sesame seeds. Heat in a slow oven until toast crisps and seeds brown.

Or serve the crab alone in its steaming and seasoning sauce, and use the excess sauce as a dip for the crab meat as you eat.

2 large live Dungeness crabs (about 6 pounds total), cleaned and cracked
½ cup butter
2 cloves garlic, minced or mashed
crab butter from 2 large live Dungeness crabs
about ½ teaspoon salt
about ¼ teaspoon freshly ground black pepper
½ cup dry white table wine or dry vermouth

Scrub crab well with a brush. Heat butter in a large kettle. Stir in garlic, then crab butter, salt, pepper, and wine. Heat to bubbling. Add crab and gently stir to coat with sauce. Cover and cook over low heat for about 15 to 20 minutes and until crab turns rosy-colored; stir once or twice. Makes about 4 servings.

Wine suggestion: A tart White Pinot such as Inglenook or Charles Krug

This is Greek, from Greek-Americans in Seattle.

It is a subtle dish and makes the most of the sweetness of crab. As it cooks, the rice takes the taste of the crab; and the crab takes up a touch of the mint. The mint seasoning should be only the minutest—just an intimation, not a full taste. The crab should be barely cooked. Garnish with lemon wedges, and squeeze the juice over as you eat. Serve with finger bowls and always French-type bread. Also serve a green salad and wine (a choice of white or red).

If you cannot get live cracked crab, you can do this with cooked—but you'll have twice-cooked crab.

MINTED CRAB PILAF

2 large uncooked Dungeness crabs, cleaned and cracked
1 large onion, very finely chopped
⅓ cup olive oil
2 large ripe tomatoes, coarsely chopped (or 1 can, 1-pound size, solid-pack tomatoes)
about 2 teaspoons salt
about ½ teaspoon freshly ground black pepper
2 cups water
1 cup uncooked long-grain white rice
1 tablespoon chopped fresh mint (or 1 teaspoon crumbled dried mint)
lemon wedges
fresh mint sprigs

Scrub crab well with a brush. In a large kettle, sauté onion in olive oil until golden. Stir in tomatoes, salt, and pepper, and simmer for about 5 minutes. Add water; cover and bring to a boil. Stir in rice and mint. Cover and cook over low heat for 10 minutes. Add crab, and cook for 15 minutes more or until rice is tender. Arrange on warm serving platter or plates. Garnish with lemon wedges and mint sprigs. Makes 4 servings.

CANTONESE GINGER CRAB WITH GREEN VEGETABLES

San Francisco Cantonese usually steam their crabs. This is one of their simple, subtle ways. Serve with steamed white rice if you wish.

2 medium-size live Dungeness crabs (about 4 pounds total), cleaned and cracked
4 tablespoons peanut oil
3 large cloves garlic, minced or mashed
1 tablespoon finely minced fresh ginger
about 1½ teaspoons salt
1 teaspoon *each* sugar and monosodium glutamate
4 green onions with green tops, halved lengthwise and cut into 3-inch lengths

½ pound fresh Chinese pea pods (or 1 package, 7 ounces, frozen Chinese pea pods) or about ¾ pound fresh mustard greens, stems removed
1 cup chicken broth
crab butter from 2 crabs
1 tablespoon *each* cornstarch and water
2 tablespoons dry sherry
1 egg, slightly beaten
Chinese parsley, finely chopped and in sprigs

Scrub crab well. In a large frying pan or kettle, heat oil over high heat; stir in garlic, ginger, salt, sugar, and monosodium glutamate. Add onions and pea pods and stir quickly to coat with oil. Stir in chicken broth and crab butter. Add crabs. Cover and cook over high heat for 5 minutes. Stir together cornstarch, water, and sherry to make a smooth paste; add to crab. Cook and stir until cornstarch mixture clears and thickens slightly. Add egg and stir just until egg sets. Turn into serving compote. Garnish with Chinese parsley. Serve immediately. Makes 3 to 4 servings.

54

For this salad, you wilt soft leaf lettuce with a bubbling browned butter. That same butter is, for the crab in the salad, the winsome seafood lemon butter. Toss this salad and serve it while hot—as a first-course or a luncheon salad.

CRAB OUT OF THE SHELL

BROWN-BUTTERED WILTED LETTUCE WITH CRAB AND ALMONDS

1 bunch leaf lettuce (about 2 quarts loosely packed torn lettuce)
1 tablespoon finely snipped chives about ⅛ teaspoon *each* salt and freshly ground black pepper
1 pound (about 2 cups) Dungeness crab meat
6 tablespoons sliced or diced toasted almonds
½ cup butter
2 teaspoons fresh lemon juice

Tear lettuce coarsely into salad bowl. Sprinkle with chives, salt, pepper, crab, and almonds. In a small frying pan, heat butter over medium heat until it foams and browns deeply; add lemon juice. Pour foaming butter over salad ingredients. Toss lightly. Serve immediately. Makes 6 first-course or 4 luncheon salads.

A CRAB SALAD

Mrs. Louis Pelfini sells poultry right next to the man who sells crab at a rambling big San Francisco market. So she is in line for the freshest crab, and at a price not quite so high as others pay. What's more, she prizes the body meat most for flavor and tenderness, whereas most outside buyers suffer under the misconception that the leg meat is best. She takes home a bounteous supply of the juicy body meat and makes her crab salad "just by putting things together more or less to taste."

It is not an exotic recipe that makes for the devastating results, but a lot of that fresh, fresh Dungeness crab in proportion to other ingredients. (That, simply, is the secret of what makes a crab salad wonderful.)

A sweet, pickle-flavored Louis dressing is a more famous crab salad topping, but Mrs. Pelfini's oil and vinegar is more suited to delicate crab.

½ cup olive oil
2 tablespoons mayonnaise
4 tablespoons wine vinegar
salt
freshly ground black pepper
1 pound (about 2 cups) fresh crab meat
½ cup finely sliced celery
2 tablespoons finely sliced green onions with part of the green tops
crisp salad greens
avocado slices, tomato wedges, and hard-cooked egg slices for garnish
chopped fresh parsley

Beat olive oil and mayonnaise together with a fork; then beat in vinegar and ¾ teaspoon salt and ¼ teaspoon pepper to make a dressing. Toss crab, celery, and green onions with a generous amount of dressing. Season with additional salt and generously with pepper to taste. Line serving platter or plates with lettuce leaves; arrange salad on top. Garnish generously with avocado slices, tomato wedges, and egg slices. Sprinkle with parsley. Pass remaining dressing. Makes 3 luncheon or supper salads or 6 first-course salads.

In 1915 someone at the San Francisco Palace Hotel created Green Goddess Dressing to honor George Arliss, then opening in William Archer's play "The Green Goddess."

Since then, the dressing has been applied to a great range of salads, most of them consisting of salad greens with crab. Still, the most popular medium for the dressing seems to be a tossed salad of broken romaine and a lot of fresh Dungeness crab meat.

CRAB WITH GREEN GODDESS DRESSING

cut clove of garlic
about 2 quarts broken romaine
   (loosely pack to measure)
1 pound (about 2 cups)
   Dungeness crab meat
Green Goddess dressing
   (recipe below)

Rub large salad bowl with garlic. Add romaine and crab. Toss gently with a generous amout of dressing. Pass additional dressing. Makes about 4 luncheon salads.

Green Goddess Dressing: Mix together thoroughly 2 cups mayonnaise; 3 tablespoons white wine vinegar; 6 anchovy fillets, very finely minced; ¼ cup finely snipped chives; ¼ cup finely chopped fresh parsley; and 2 tablespoons minced fresh tarragon (or 1 tablespoon crumbled dried tarragon). Cover and chill for 30 minutes or more before serving.

CRAB AND EGGPLANT CHABLIS

6 tablespoons butter
1 small unpeeled eggplant (less than 1 pound), cut into ¾-inch cubes
about ¼ teaspoon salt
Chablis Béchamel sauce (recipe below)

1 pound (about 2 cups) Dungeness crab meat
¼ pound (about 1 cup) tiny shrimp
⅓ cup grated Parmesan cheese
6 buttered toasted brioche shells or crisp popovers broken open

Melt butter in a large frying pan. Add eggplant, sprinkle with salt, and sauté over medium-high heat until golden and just tender. Fold eggplant into Chablis Béchamel along with crab and shrimp. Turn into a buttered baking dish (about 2 quarts). Sprinkle with Parmesan. Bake in a moderate oven (350°) for 30 minutes or until bubbling. Serve over brioche shells or popovers. Makes 6 servings.

Chablis Béchamel: In a saucepan, melt 6 tablespoons butter and stir in 6 tablespoons flour and ¾ teaspoon salt to make a smooth paste. Gradually add 2 cups half and half (half milk and half cream), cooking and stirring until sauce is smooth and thickened. Remove from heat and stir in 1 cup California Chablis or other dry white table wine, ½ teaspoon crumbled dried basil, ⅛ teaspoon ground nutmeg, ⅓ cup grated Parmesan cheese, and ¼ cup finely chopped fresh parsley.

Wine suggestion: A California Chablis such as Inglenook White Pinot

Serve this crab-lavish sauce spooned into crisp, opened popovers, or tender brioches that have been broken open, hollowed out, brushed with butter, and lightly toasted. (You can make popovers ahead, then return them to a hot oven for 5 minutes just before serving to reheat and crisp.)

You can assemble the casserole hours before serving time, cover and chill, and bake just in time to serve.

That lyrically gentle steamed custard of the Japanese, Chawan Mushi, has taken on a fragile Western flavor as Japanese cooks here have introduced Dungeness crab into it. They put flakes of white crab meat into their broth-egg custard to enrich it or to replace some of the traditional suspended bits of filling—a pea, a shrimp, a bit of chicken, a dried mushroom, pieces of white fish.

It is surprising that Chawan Mushi can be so easy to make when the results are so sublime. Put this together and start to steam just 20 minutes before serving; it will begin to weep if you try to hold it. Serve it as a first course before a broiled meat.

Or Chawan Mushi can be the main course for a brunch or luncheon. Tea or sake and sesame wafers are good with it. Chilled mandarin oranges make a subtle fruit counterpoint to the custard, as dessert or served alongside.

59

CRAB CHAWAN MUSHI

4 eggs
about 4 cups mildly seasoned
    chicken stock, fat removed
1 teaspoon sweet sake or sherry
½ teaspoon soy sauce
⅛ teaspoon *each* salt and
    monosodium glutamate
12 one-inch sprigs of watercress
8 thin slices lemon peel
4 small crab legs
6 tablespoons flaked crab meat

Beat eggs lightly, just until whites and yolks are thoroughly mixed. Measure beaten eggs, and add 4 times their quantity of stock. Add sake, soy, salt, and monosodium glutamate, and mix well. Divide watercress, lemon peel, and crab among 4 custard or soup cups (about 1¼-cup size). Pour egg mixture into cups. Cover each with foil or loosely with its own lid. Place on a rack in a large kettle above gently boiling water. Cover kettle and steam custards for 20 minutes or until knife inserted near center comes out clean (cut through foil). Serve immediately. Makes 4 servings.

FISHERMAN'S CRAB ON SPAGHETTINI

The cooking is so slight you can do this in a chafing dish in front of your guests. Be sure not to overdo the A.1. sauce.

¼ cup butter
½ pound Dungeness crab meat
¼ pound tiny shrimp
¼ cup brandy
⅓ cup commercial sour cream
¼ cup Hollandaise sauce
   (recipe page 105)
1 teaspoon *each* Worcestershire
   and A.1. sauce
few drops liquid hot-pepper seasoning
3 tablespoons chopped fresh parsley
freshly ground black pepper
about 6 ounces spaghettini or
   vermicelli, cooked *al dente*
grated Parmesan cheese

Melt butter over low heat in a large frying pan or chafing dish. Add crab and shrimp, and turn to coat with butter. Add brandy at edge of pan, and as soon as it warms, light it. Stir shellfish gently with brandy until flames die. Add sour cream, Hollandaise, Worcestershire, A.1., liquid hot-pepper seasoning, parsley, and a generous grinding of black pepper. Stir gently to mix and heat through. Serve over hot spaghettini that has been placed on 3 warm serving plates. Grind on additional pepper. Sprinkle lightly with Parmesan. Makes 3 servings.

Wine suggestion: Louis Martini Gewürz Traminer

CHAPTER 4
GINGER AND FISH

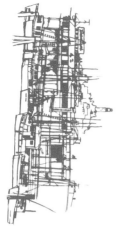

Confucius in his wisdom is said to have always had ginger at his table. By Chinese tradition, ginger imparts a fountain-of-youth quality to whatever it spices and to whoever eats it.

It may be because of these advantages—or an independent fact—but Chinese cooks hardly ever cook fish without ginger; they use it as a "de-fisher"—to cut fish-oil flavors without destroying sweet sea flavors. Japanese fish cooks use ginger as consistently as the Chinese, because of ginger's warm flavor and hot bite.

At any rate, ginger is to the Oriental fish cook the constant spicing that lemon is to the fish cooks of most other cuisines.

And the ginger flavor enhancement that applies to fish cookery also applies to the accompaniments that go with fish. Something gingery eaten along with fish, such as a ginger-spiced bread or ginger-seasoned vegetables, can enhance the taste of the fish in almost the same way as ginger cooked with the fish.

The recipes in this chapter document that seafood-ginger affinity. They come from the cooks of San Francisco's Chinatown, from the West Coast Japanese from Seattle to San Diego, and from Occidental good cooks up and down the Coast who have gleaned the fish-and-ginger wisdom from their Oriental friends. (See also these seafood-and-ginger recipes elsewhere in the book: Cantonese Ginger Crab with Green Vegetables, page 54 ; Apricot Prawn Sauté, page 24 ; and Sweet and Sour Fish, The Mandarin, page 109.)

The Oriental's choice form of ginger is obviously fresh ginger root; but other cooks use other forms—dried, ground, preserved, crystallized, canned—satisfactorily. To store fresh ginger, just put it in your freezer unwrapped; the outer skin provides sufficient packaging. Use ginger directly as it comes from the freezer; it thaws rapidly. Or mince or grate it while frozen.

CHINATOWN RAW FISH SALAD

¾ pound fillet of sea bass, cod, or rockfish
4 tablespoons sesame seed oil
about ¾ teaspoon salt
about ½ teaspoon freshly ground black pepper
¼ teaspoon sugar
1/16 teaspoon ground cinnamon
1 tablespoon very fine slivers of preserved sweet cucumbers
1 tablespoon very fine slivers of preserved red ginger
1 tablespoon minced preserved ginger (the familiar gold-colored kind available in most supermarkets)
3 green onions (white part only), cut into 2-inch lengths and slivered lengthwise
4 tablespoons finely chopped salted peanuts
snowy rice sticks (directions below)
about ⅓ cup fine sprigs of Chinese parsley
1 lemon, cut in half

If necessary, remove skin and bones from fish. Cut flesh into very thin strips. Toss with sesame oil, salt, pepper, sugar, and cinnamon, and allow to marinate for 5 minutes. Drain off any excess marinade. Toss fish lightly with cucumbers, red ginger, preserved ginger, and onions; arrange in a shallow serving platter. Just before serving, sprinkle with peanuts, snowy rice sticks, and Chinese parsley. Put a half lemon at each end of platter. Squeeze all the lemon juice over as you eat. Makes 2 generous servings.

Snowy rice sticks: Heat about 1 inch salad oil in a small pan over medium-high heat. Add 1 to 2 ounces Chinese fine rice sticks, a few at a time, and fry until they puff and turn white. Remove from oil with slotted spoon; crumble slightly.

In San Francisco's Chinatown, many people know this hot-and-cold ginger salad as Sam Wo's salad because the little hole-in-the-wall, upstairs-above-the-kitchen restaurant by that name is famous for it. There it is usually of smelt instead of rockfish or cod or bass.

This is one time when there is no substitute for Chinese parsley (fresh coriander). If you can't get it after scouring your Oriental, Spanish, Mexican, and Portuguese markets and if you don't grow it, don't bother with this recipe. Any substitutes are too much of a compromise.

This whole recipe depends upon a successful marketing trip to a Chinatown. The fish must be ultra-fresh.

"Cantonese" when applied to a lobster, crab, or prawn dish means black-bean-seasoned. The Cantonese count garlic as a "de-fisher" almost as much as ginger; and garlic invariably goes with black beans.

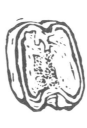

LOBSTER WITH BLACK BEAN SAUCE (LOBSTER CANTONESE)

1 pound spiny lobster tails
2 teaspoons fermented black beans
   (also called preserved black beans
   or black salted beans;
   Dow See in Cantonese)
2 large cloves garlic, peeled
1 teaspoon minced fresh ginger
2 tablespoons soy sauce
½ teaspoon sugar
2 tablespoons peanut oil
   (or other light salad oil)

2 ounces ground or minced pork
6 tablespoons boiling water
2 teaspoons cornstarch mixed to a
   smooth paste with 1 tablespoon
   cold water
2 tablespoons finely chopped
   green bell peppers
1 egg, slightly beaten

Thaw frozen lobster tails. Cut away and remove under shells. If 6 ounces or larger, split through shell lengthwise. Wash black beans thoroughly in cold running water; drain well. Crush black beans with 1 of the large garlic cloves; mix in ginger, soy, and sugar. Heat oil over high heat in a large heavy frying pan. Add the remaining whole garlic clove and pork, and brown quickly; discard garlic. Add lobster and water, and spoon black bean mixture over exposed lobster flesh. Cover and cook over medium-high heat for 6 minutes or until lobster loses translucency. Add cornstarch paste and heat and stir until it coats lobster. Add green pepper and egg; heat and stir just until egg sets. Serve immediately. Makes 2 main-dish servings.

GREEN PEPPER BAKED BASS WITH PUMPKIN GINGERBREAD

3 large onions, thinly sliced
2 green bell peppers, seeded and cut into sliver strips
2 stalks celery, chopped
3 tablespoons butter
2 large ripe tomatoes, peeled and chopped
salt and freshly ground black pepper
whole striped bass (about 6 pounds), cleaned and head removed
4 lemons, thinly sliced

In a large frying pan, sauté half the onions, half the green peppers, and half the celery in butter until limp. Add tomatoes and about ½ teaspoon salt and ¼ teaspoon pepper. Cook over medium heat for about 10 minutes; stir occasionally. Rub fish inside and out generously with salt and pepper. Fill cavity with remaining onions, peppers, and celery, and with half the lemon slices; skewer shut. Place in a buttered shallow baking pan and arrange remaining lemon slices over the top. Spoon tomato sauce over. Bake in a moderate oven (350°) for 40 minutes or until fish flakes with a fork. Spoon pan juices over fish servings. Makes about 8 servings.

Pumpkin gingerbread: In a mixing bowl, cream together 1½ cups sugar and ½ cup salad oil. Beat in 2 eggs thoroughly. Sift together 2⅔ cups unsifted all-purpose flour, 1 teaspoon soda, ¾ teaspoon salt, ¼ teaspoon baking powder, 1 teaspoon ground ginger, and ½ teaspoon each ground cinnamon, nutmeg, cloves, and allspice; add to creamed mixture alternately with ⅓ cup water. Beat in ½ can (1-pound size) pumpkin (about 1 cup). Turn into a greased 5-by-9-inch loaf pan. Bake in a moderate oven (350°) for 1 hour or until toothpick inserted in center comes out clean. Allow to cool in pan for about 10 minutes; then turn out on wire rack to cool thoroughly. Makes 1 loaf.

The ginger spicing in the bread has the hotness you would want in the fish seasoning if it weren't in the accompanying bread.

Carve the bread into thick slices, butter, and broil-toast so it will be crisp to eat with the fish.

Lacking a whole striped bass, you can apply this treatment to two thick fillets (about 1¼ pounds each) of sea bass or other fleshy white fish, baked one on top of another with stuffing between. Bake as below, for about 40 minutes.

The interior fish stuffing is for flavoring, not eating.

Unhappily Monterey is no longer the first fishing area of California. Time was when the Chinese, then the Italians, and later the Japanese made a prosperous living from the sardine, mackerel, and abalone fishing off the Monterey coast. But there came a change, and the fish aren't so plentiful as they once were.

The big change came around 1947 to 1949, when the sardines suddenly disappeared; and a big fishing industry likewise disappeared. Fishermen argue the reasons—a change in the current, the Bomb, overfishing, shortage of fish food supply. But no matter why, the sardines haven't returned.

Traditionally a fishing town, Monterey is still that, but now on a smaller scale and now more for fish eating than for fish catching.

Ken Sato is sort of a "Mr. Seafood"

of Monterey. He imports and exports fish, loves to eat them, fishes for sport, and knows all the fish people as friends.

His wife cooks fish the way he likes it, honoring a Japanese fish-cooking rule: Have the sauce boiling before you add the fish.

SATO'S GINGER COD

¼ cup soy sauce
¼ cup sake or dry sherry
3 tablespoons sugar
1 teaspoon minced fresh ginger
4 one-inch-thick steaks of lingcod, about 2 pounds total (or use other good-size fleshy fish such as cod or sea bass)
1 green onion with part of green top, very thinly sliced

Combine soy, sake, sugar, and ginger in a frying pan or kettle with cover, and bring to a boil. Add fish, arranging it in a single layer, cover, and simmer for 5 minutes. Turn fish over, cover, and simmer for 5 minutes more or just until flesh loses translucency and flakes with a fork. Serve fish in rimmed plates, with juices poured over. Sprinkle with onions. Makes 4 servings.

GIANT PRAWNS TERIYAKI

Also important in Monterey to anyone serious about seafood is the Ginza Restaurant, where the special-occasion, order-ahead Teriyaki Prawns are served with their charcoal-broiled-on teriyaki glaze.

The problem in reproducing the Ginza prawns is getting the giant-size, almost lobsterlike prawns. The prawns should be five-to-seven-count size (five to seven per pound), and such prawns are so sought after by the restaurant trade that they are rare in retail markets. But they are worth pursuing with your fish man; or use the largest prawns you can find.

2 pounds very large prawns
   (about 12)
¾ cup soy sauce
½ cup sake or dry sherry
6 tablespoons sugar
¼ cup salad oil
2 cloves garlic, minced or mashed
1 teaspoon grated fresh ginger
1 teaspoon monosodium glutamate

Shell and devein prawns, leaving tail shells on. Combine remaining ingredients in a bowl; add prawns, and marinate at room temperature for 1 hour; turn occasionally. Remove prawns from marinade and place on well-greased grill over low charcoal; broil on both sides until prawns turn pink, lose translucence, and acquire a glaze, about 6 minutes each side. Baste frequently with marinade. Makes 4 servings.

Serve as a condiment accompaniment to fish. Excellent with something like swordfish grilled over charcoal and sprinkled with soy sauce.

JOHNNY GOTA'S SALAD RELISH FOR FISH

2 carrots
2 cucumbers
2 teaspoons salt
ginger dressing (recipe below)

Peel carrots and cucumbers and cut into very thin diagonal slices. Sprinkle with salt, toss, and let stand for 5 minutes. Rinse with cold water and drain well; pour ginger dressing over and serve. Makes 4 servings.

Ginger dressing: Stir together ½ cup white wine vinegar, ¼ cup sugar, ¼ cup darkly toasted sesame seeds, 1 teaspoon salt, ½ teaspoon monosodium glutamate, 2 teaspoons minced fresh ginger, and 4 green onions with part of green tops, minced. Note: To toast sesame seeds, sprinkle on baking sheet and brown well in a moderate (350°) oven; stir or shake occasionally.

STEAMED SHRIMP TANGERINE

This recipe illustrates just how exotic West Coast cuisine can be. Armenian Elise Kazanjian borrowed from the Japanese and invented this when her husband had to cut down on the oils in his diet.

about 2 tablespoons salad oil
3 cakes *tofu* (soy bean cake or curd, *Dow Foo* in Chinese), cut into 1- to 2-inch squares
6 large dried black mushrooms, soaked in warm water for 1 hour, squeezed dry, and thinly sliced
1 pound medium-size raw shrimp, peeled and deveined
1 tablespoon fermented black beans, very well washed and drained

about 1 teaspoon grated fresh ginger
1½-inch square of dried tangerine peel, soaked in warm water for 30 minutes and minced
2 green onions with part of green tops, minced
2 tablespoons soy sauce
1 teaspoon monosodium glutamate
½ teaspoon cornstarch
hot steamed white rice

Heat oil over medium-high heat in a frying pan; add tofu squares, and lightly brown on both sides; remove from pan. Add mushrooms to pan, and sauté just until lightly browned. Arrange tofu and mushrooms over bottom of a serving platter. Sprinkle with shrimp. Mash together black beans, ginger, and tangerine peel; stir in onions; sprinkle over shrimp. Mix soy, monosodium glutamate, and cornstarch, and pour over all. Place platter on rack in a large kettle or steamer above boiling water. Cover and steam for 8 to 10 minutes, until shrimp turn pink and lose translucency. Serve over rice. Makes 3 to 4 servings.

The freshest and lightest kind of sweet and sour sauce makes a warm glaze for poached fish.

You can use fish steaks or fillets in the same way as a whole piece, but poach for a shorter time, about 8 minutes.

POACHED FISH SPICED WITH AMBER SAUCE

2-pound piece lingcod, rockfish, sea bass, sturgeon, or salmon
court bouillon (recipe below)
½ cup brown sugar, firmly packed
¼ cup white wine vinegar
¼ cup seedless raisins
4 gingersnaps, crushed to crumbs
2 teaspoons scraped onion juice
1 lemon, very thinly sliced and seeded
½ teaspoon salt

Wrap fish in cheesecloth. Lower into simmering court bouillon. Cover, return to simmering, and simmer until fish flakes with a fork, about 20 minutes. Gently lift fish from bouillon, unwrap, remove skin, and place on warm serving platter. Strain court bouillon; measure 1 cup into a saucepan. Add to saucepan brown sugar, vinegar, raisins, gingersnap crumbs, onion juice, lemon, and salt; cook over medium-high heat, stirring, until smooth and thickened, about 3 minutes. Pour sauce over fish. Makes 4 servings.

Court bouillon: Combine in a kettle (deep enough so liquid will just cover fish) 6 cups water; 1 onion, sliced; 1 whole lemon, sliced; 2 stalks celery with leaves; 1 bay leaf; 6 whole allspice; 6 whole peppercorns; and ½ teaspoon salt. Cover, bring to a boil, then simmer for 5 minutes.

FREDI'S GINGER CLAM PILAF

The ginger is slight but significant. With this serve dark beer, a tossed green salad with chopped dill pickles in it, dark sour rye bread, and salted butter.

1 cup uncooked long-grain white rice
1½ tablespoons salad oil
4 slices bacon, cut into small pieces
¾ cup chopped celery
1 small onion, finely chopped
½ large green bell pepper, chopped
2 cans (about 7 ounces *each*) minced clams with liquor
½ can (6-ounce size) tomato paste
1 can (2½ ounces) sliced black olives, drained
1 cup chicken stock
1 large ripe tomato, peeled, seeded and chopped

¼ cup dry vermouth
1½ tablespoons fresh lemon juice
1 teaspoon brown sugar
1 teaspoon finely minced fresh ginger or about ½ teaspoon ground ginger
½ teaspoon *each* crumbled dried thyme and tarragon
about ¼ teaspoon *each* salt and freshly ground black pepper
1 small clove garlic, minced or mashed
¾ cup sliced almonds, toasted

In a large heavy frying pan, sauté rice in oil over medium heat, stirring, until it is well browned and begins to pop. In a 2- to 2½-quart casserole (or in a frying pan), cook bacon slowly until some fat accumulates; add celery, onion, and green pepper, and sauté until limp. Drain off any excess fat. Add browned rice along with remaining ingredients, except almonds; mix thoroughly. (Transfer to a casserole if necessary.) Bake, uncovered, in a moderate oven (350°) for 45 minutes or until rice is just tender. Sprinkle almonds around edge as a border. Makes 6 servings.

Note: To toast almonds, sprinkle on baking sheet; lightly brown in a moderate oven (350°); stir or shake occasionally.

The late Helen Evans Brown developed this sesame broiling for sea bass. James Beard reported it in his fish-cookery book and generously grants it another exposure.

SEA BASS SESAME

2 **pounds fillet of sea bass**
3 **cloves garlic, minced or mashed**
2 **teaspoons salt**
6 **tablespoons melted butter**
3 **tablespoons bourbon or Scotch
   whisky or brandy**
3 **tablespoons fresh lemon juice**
2 **tablespoons soy sauce**
1½ **teaspoons minced fresh ginger**
½ **cup sesame seeds**
lime or lemon wedges

Wipe fish with a damp cloth. Mash garlic and salt together to a paste and rub over both sides of fish. Let stand for 1 hour or more. Combine butter, bourbon, lemon juice, soy, ginger, and sesame seeds; brush over both sides of fish. Place fish in a hinged broiler, and barbecue over moderate coals until fish flakes and sesame seeds are well toasted; turn about twice and brush frequently with remaining butter mixture. (Or broil in oven: Place fillet on greased, foil-lined, preheated broiler pan; brush top side only with butter mixture; broil about 6 to 8 inches from heat, brushing with butter mixture, until fish flakes and seeds are toasted; do not turn.) Serve with lime wedges. Makes 4 servings.

WHIPPED CREAM SALMON MOUSSE

Make this whipped-cream mousse a day ahead of serving so the flavors can mellow.

The ginger is not in the salmon but in the ginger-toasted muffins that go with the salmon: Serve mousse for a salad luncheon and accompany with hot English muffins that have been split, buttered with a mixture of four tablespoons soft butter to two teaspoons ground ginger, and broil-toasted until crisp.

2 envelopes unflavored gelatin
½ cup water
2 tablespoons *each* white wine vinegar, fresh lemon juice, and catsup
⅛ teaspoon freshly ground black pepper
1 cup mayonnaise
1 large can (1 pound) red salmon, drained, skin removed, and finely flaked
½ cup (about 20) pimento-stuffed olives, finely chopped
2 hard-cooked eggs, finely chopped
2 teaspoons minced sweet pickle
1 cup heavy cream, whipped
crisp lettuce leaves, lemon wedges, additional olives, hard-cooked-egg wedges for garnish

Soften gelatin in water in top part of double boiler; heat over hot water until dissolved. Combine dissolved gelatin thoroughly with remaining ingredients, except cream and garnish. Fold in whipped cream. Turn into a lightly oiled 1½-quart mold (or individual molds). Cover and chill for at least 24 hours. Unmold on lettuce-lined salad platter or plates. Garnish with lemon, olives, and eggs. Makes 8 servings.

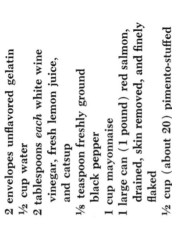

72

Drop this on top of hot broiled or poached fish for a plush saucing.

GINGER BROWN-BUTTER MAYONNAISE

1 cup butter
4 egg yolks
2 teaspoons ground ginger

Heat butter over medium heat until it foams and is richly browned, stirring occasionally. Remove from heat and allow to cool to lukewarm. Put egg yolks in blender container and whirl for a few seconds to blend, then add butter (through opening in blender top) in a small, slow, steady stream. Add ginger and whirl until thickened and blended. Makes about 1 cup, topping for about 8 servings.

CHAPTER 5

SHELLFISH AND SHERRY

The Spanish started it; Californians continued it: honoring the remarkable affinity of shellfish and sherry.

In Spanish coastal towns, *tapa* time means drinking dry sherry and eating local shellfish—shrimp, prawns, lobster. The two sensations interlock perfectly. It is unthinkable to sever them. To the Spanish, shellfish and sherry are bound together more closely than port and Stilton to an Englishman or bock beer and spring sausage to a Bavarian.

That Spanish taste suggestion is too good to be ignored; and Californians haven't. We link our own fine California sherries with shellfish in cooking as well as in pure forms. It is following a Spanish suggestion that we serve dry sherry as an apéritif, along with broiled shrimp or cracked crab. The Spanish know that their driest sherries are dry enough for a table wine; and Californians serve dry sherry and a hot crab bisque laced with sherry as a first course, or dry sherry and a first-course salad of greens and shellfish with a sherry-seasoned dressing. For a soup supper we have a shellfish-rich soup, sherry, and bread. It is by augmenting the Spanish suggestion that we sometimes use the shellfish-sherry link in cooking only, as seasoning a shellfish sauce or a casserole or a sauté with sherry, and drinking another wine.

The recipes in this chapter look at Western shellfish from the sherry perspective. They demonstrate what an institution the combination has quietly come to be.

These garlic-broiled shrimp are so Spanish in theme that you almost have to have sherry with them at cocktail time.

If you serve them as appetizers at a morning barbecue brunch, cut back on the garlic a little and serve another Spanish drink, Andaluz: Combine equal parts dry sherry and orange juice. Chill thoroughly or serve over ice.

GARLIC-BROILED SPANISH SHRIMP

1½ pounds large raw shrimp (about 12-to-15-per-pound size)
½ cup olive oil
¼ cup dry sherry
1 clove garlic, minced or mashed
4 tablespoons finely minced parsley
about ½ teaspoon salt
about ¼ teaspoon freshly ground black pepper
⅛ teaspoon crumbled dried thyme
⅛ teaspoon crushed dried red peppers

Shell and devein shrimp, leaving tail shells on. Mix remaining ingredients in a bowl, add shrimp, and marinate for 1 hour or more; turn occasionally. Broil shrimp on both sides over low charcoal (or in oven broiler, placed about 6 inches from heat) until shrimp turn pink and lose translucence, about 4 minutes each side. Baste occasionally with marinade. (Or melt about 2 tablespoons butter in a frying pan over low heat, add shrimp in sauce, and cook until shrimp are pink and opaque, about 6 minutes.) Makes appetizers for about 6 people.

PARSLEY-CRAB CANAPÉS FOR SHERRY

½ pound (about 1 cup) flaked
   crab meat
3 tablespoons finely chopped
   fresh parsley
1 teaspoon fresh lemon juice
about 2 tablespoons mayonnaise

salt
freshly ground black pepper
about 8 two-inch rounds of
   thin, firm white bread,
   generously buttered
parsley sprigs

Toss crab meat and parsley with lemon juice, enough mayonnaise to moisten well, and salt and a generous amount of pepper to taste. Pile on buttered bread. Garnish with parsley. Makes about 8 generous canapés.

This is a luxurious canapé, explicitly to go with dry sherry at tea time or before dinner. It is beguiling because of its simplicity, its deep mounding of crab meat, and the wondrous alchemy of shellfish and sherry.

Dungeness crab is the choicest crab to use.

Get the biggest prawns or other shrimp-like crustaceans in the market for this. They should be at least eight-to-ten-count size (eight to ten per pound). If you can get larger prawns, plan on about two pounds for four servings, and follow recipe proportions below.

These are also good to serve as hors d'oeuvres with dry sherry.

CRAB-STUFFED PRAWNS, SHERRY ROASTED

16 very large prawns (8-to-10-count)
½ cup dry sherry
¼ cup salad oil
2 tablespoons minced shallots
1 teaspoon dry mustard
1 teaspoon crumbled dried tarragon
½ teaspoon crumbled dried thyme
¼ teaspoon freshly ground
    black pepper
½ pound crab meat, finely flaked
16 thin slices bacon

Shell and devein prawns, leaving tail shells on. With a sharp knife, carefully cut deeper into vein line of each prawn, over halfway through meat. Combine sherry, oil, shallots, mustard, tarragon, thyme, and pepper in a bowl; add prawns and marinate at room temperature for 1 hour; turn occasionally. Remove from marinade, and fill back opening of each prawn with part of the crab meat; spiral-wrap with bacon to hold crab in place. Place prawns on wire rack set over a shallow pan, and bake in a hot oven (425°) for 15 minutes or just until bacon is crisp. Makes 4 generous servings.

SHERRY CRAB IN CREAM–PARMESAN POPOVERS

Sherry is for saucing and for sipping. Serve this as a rich dinner first course with dry sherry.

¼ cup butter
1 pound (about 2 cups, firmly packed) crab meat
½ cup heavy (whipping) cream
¼ cup dry sherry
¼ cup finely chopped fresh parsley
¼ teaspoon crumbled dried chervil
about ¼ teaspoon *each* salt and freshly ground black pepper
Parmesan popovers (recipe below) (or pastry cups or triangles or toast points)

Melt butter in a frying pan. Add crab, and gently turn, to coat with butter. Add cream, sherry, parsley, chervil, and salt and pepper to taste. Heat to bubbling and simmer for 2 minutes. Serve over hot popovers, broken open. Makes 6 servings.

Parmesan popovers: Beat together with rotary beater 2 eggs, 1 cup milk, and 2 tablespoons grated Parmesan cheese. Sift 1 cup flour with ½ teaspoon salt into milk mixture. Beat until smooth; do not overbeat. Pour into 6 well-buttered 5- or 6-ounce custard cups, deep muffin tins, or popover pans. Bake in a hot oven (425°) for 30 minutes or until puffed and golden brown. Serve immediately. Makes 6 popovers.

This is one of those recipes that has been passed around from good cook to good cook—always with incredulity registered that it could be so simple. Even those who don't believe in canned-soup soups like this. It is just too easy and delicious not to include.

The two soups, tomato and pea, are basic to the recipe. But beyond that, the changes cooks make are countless—the kind of wine for marinating, no marinating, a pinch of curry, a touch of basil, a sprinkling of Parmesan, part shrimp, part lobster . . .

This is one of the first versions and still about the best. The subtle sherry in the soup calls for the fullness of sherry as a beverage.

SHERRIED CRAB BISQUE

½ pound (about 1 cup)
   flaked crab meat
½ cup dry sherry
1 can (about 10 ounces) tomato soup
1 can (about 10 ounces) green
   pea soup
1¼ cups half and half
   (half milk, half cream)
about ¾ teaspoon curry powder
chopped fresh parsley
   and/or paprika

Marinate crab in sherry for about 30 minutes. In a saucepan, blend together undiluted tomato and pea soups, half and half, and curry. Heat slowly, stirring; do not boil. Add crab and sherry and heat through. Serve immediately, sprinkled lightly with parsley and/or paprika. Makes 6 first-course servings, 4 supper servings.

All up and down the Western fishing coast, the families who have been the fishermen continue to be the fishermen. They often branch out their operations to wholesale markets, retail markets, and fish restaurants. This story of progress is repeated over and over by hard-working fisher families—often Scandinavians and Slavs in the northwest, Genoese around San Francisco, Japanese and Sicilians around Monterey, and Portuguese and Italians in the south.

Italian George Castagnola is a part of such a story in Santa Barbara. He overwhelms you with his exuberance about life and fish. If you're interested in fish, you're immediately a compagno of his.

Along with the fishing and fish-marketing business, he has master-minded the handsome Harbor Restaurant, where you can wine and seafood-dine over the water and in a setting of authentic ship-wood decor.

Frank Chellond, the executive chef of the Harbor, does this sherry-and-butter mingling to get a glossy amber glaze on scallops. He suggests accompaniments: crumb-topped baked tomatoes, little brown-roasted potatoes, a dry white wine.

SHERRY GLAZED SCALLOPS ON LEAF SPINACH

1 pound fresh scallops
salt and freshly ground black pepper
flour
¼ cup butter
¼ cup finely minced shallots
¾ cup dry sherry
about 2½ pounds fresh spinach (or 2
    packages, *each* about 12
    ounces, frozen leaf spinach),
    cooked and seasoned with butter,
    salt, and pepper

Rinse and dry scallops thoroughly. Cut into about 1-inch pieces. Season well with salt and pepper. Coat lightly with flour. Melt butter in a large frying pan over medium-high heat. Stir in shallots to coat with butter, then push to edge of pan. Add scallops (only enough to cover bottom of pan without crowding) and sauté until golden brown on both sides, about 4 minutes total. Add sherry, and cook, gently stirring, until juices are reduced to a glaze. Arrange scallops on top of hot spinach. Makes 4 servings.

KING CRAB WITH SUPPER EGGS

Jerry DiVecchio is one of the most food-creative young hostesses, home-makers, and food writers in California. This is one of her ravishing shellfish-and-egg table cookery ideas.

She suggests cooking it before your guest(s) in a frying pan set over an alcohol flame—after browning onions in the kitchen ("'Course the time it takes the onions to cook is just long enough for a nice little cocktail"). Or cook it entirely in the kitchen. But wherever, serve from your presentable frying pan.

A caution: Don't stir the eggs too much and lose the pretty red of the crab.

This serves two hungry adults (especially satisfying late at night)—with a little lettuce salad and sourdough bread and perhaps dry sherry.

1 large white onion, very thinly sliced	1 to 2 tablespoons chopped fresh parsley
4 tablespoons butter	½ pound large pieces of frozen, thawed King crab
4 tablespoons dry sherry	4 eggs
salt	1 tablespoon water
about ¼ pound small whole mushrooms (or larger mushrooms cut into halves or quarters)	

In a wide frying pan (9-to-10-inch diameter), slowly cook onions with 1 tablespoon of the butter and 2 tablespoons of the sherry, stirring frequently, until onions become light golden brown and slightly crisp, at least 20 minutes. Turn out of pan, salt lightly to taste, and keep warm. Melt another 1 tablespoon butter in frying pan and add the remaining sherry and mushrooms, and cook quickly, stirring or shaking pan, until mushrooms are lightly browned and liquid evaporates. Turn mushrooms out of pan and keep warm. Melt remaining 2 tablespoons butter in frying pan over low heat, add parsley, and stir to coat with butter. Add crab, and heat for about 1 minute (do not stir; take care to keep pieces whole). Beat eggs with water and about ½ teaspoon salt; pour around, not over, crab in pan. Cook over low heat, slipping a wide spatula gently under set eggs, letting liquid egg flow to pan bottom. (Keep crab exposed and whole.) When eggs are barely set (still moist-looking on top), sprinkle hot mushrooms over the top, and make a border of the hot onions. Serve from frying pan.

You are the lobster meat up over its own shell to perch it on a natural pedestal for this presentation. The lobster is handsome-looking, and the meat is out of the shell and easy to eat.

ARCED LOBSTER WITH SHERRY MUSTARD BUTTER

4 spiny lobster tails (about 8 ounces *each*)
¾ cup butter
1½ tablespoons dry sherry
1½ tablespoons fresh lemon juice
¼ teaspoon Dijon-style mustard
grinding of black pepper (optional)

Thaw frozen lobster tails. Cut away and remove under shells. Cut away center section of tail. Gently loosen meat from shell *except* leave it attached at tail. Lift loose meat out of shell groove and place it over back of shell by gently pulling it between remaining tail sections. Slit the thin membrane covering lobster meat down center to prevent curling. Melt butter and stir in sherry, lemon juice, mustard, and pepper; brush generously over both sides of lobster meat. Place lobster in a greased shallow pan and bake in a hot oven (450°) for about 10 minutes, basting occasionally with sherry butter. Serve with remaining sherry butter as a dipping sauce. Makes 4 servings.

Shortly after the turn of the century, it was a common occurrence for Italian commercial fishermen to become Italian seafood restaurateurs. Around San Francisco Bay, present-day restaurants so started are Spenger's in Berkeley, the Sea Wolf in Jack London Square in Oakland, Castagnola's, Alioto's, DiMaggio's, Tarantino's, and Sabella's at San Francisco Fisherman's Wharf.

The same thing happened in Eureka, with Lazio's restaurant. On long summer nights, people from interior California drive for three and a half hours —from as far as Redding—to come to the Coast and have a fresh seafood dinner at Lazio's.

For eight years, Mrs. Kilpatrick has been head chef at Lazio's. And for eight years, she has made delicate crab-rich crab patties her specialty for Friday nights. She intends them as a supper main course. Paradoxically, though, their buttery rich homespunness makes them almost elegant; and they can be a lovely first course—served on small plates, garnished with lemon and parsley—with dry sherry to drink.

SHERRY CRAB PATTIES

1 pound crab meat, finely flaked
½ cup minced celery
3 tablespoons finely chopped fresh parsley
1½ tablespoons minced fresh onion
2 tablespoons cracker meal
2 eggs
2 tablespoons dry sherry
1 tablespoon milk
1 clove garlic, minced or mashed
salt
freshly ground black pepper
lemon wedges

Toss together thoroughly crab, celery, parsley, onion, and cracker meal. Beat eggs with sherry, milk, and garlic. Add to crab mixture, and mix well. Add salt if necessary and pepper to taste. Shape mixture into dollar-size patties about ½ inch thick. Heat butter about ⅛ inch deep in a large frying pan. Add patties, and sauté over medium heat just until golden on both sides; handle gently. Add more butter to pan as needed. Serve hot with lemon wedges. Makes about 8 first-course servings or 4 supper servings.

The shellfish (scallops) go into the sherry sauce just to add their sweetness, then out. Serve sauce over any fine white fish, broiled, baked, poached, or fried. Excellent on broiled true red snapper.

HEARTS OF ARTICHOKE SAUCE

4 tablespoons minced shallots
¼ pound fresh mushrooms, thinly sliced
¾ cup butter
½ pound scallops, rinsed, dried, and cut into small pieces
1 package (8 ounces) frozen artichoke hearts, thawed
4 tablespoons chopped fresh parsley
¾ cup dry sherry
2 tablespoons fresh lemon juice
½ teaspoon salt
generous grinding of black pepper

Sauté shallots and mushrooms in butter in a frying pan until tender and golden; push to side of pan. Add scallops and cook over low heat, stirring occasionally, for about 10 minutes; remove scallops. Cut artichokes into about ¼-inch-thick slices and add to frying pan, along with parsley, sherry, lemon juice, salt, and pepper. Cook over medium heat until juices reduce to a very thin sauce consistency. Makes sauce for about 6 servings of fish.

CHAPTER 6

THE RED WINE FISHES
THE EXCEPTIONS TO THE RULE

There aren't a vast number of them, but there are fish and fish dishes that are big enough that a red (or rosé) wine seems more appropriate than a white wine. They stand outside of the general rule, but for good reason.

The measure of whether to serve white wine or red is simply whether or not the fish is a big enough dish to need the force of a red wine. Some grilled or fried fish,

highly spiced fish stews, and some very fat and/or full-flavored fish are big enough. Their pungency puts them in quite another category than most fish and shellfish.

In some older cuisines, the southern cuisines of Europe, red wine with fish is a not infrequent custom. In Portugal, the famed *Caldeirada* (fishermen's stew) isn't considered at all complete without a chilled red *vinho verde* (slightly sparkling "green wine"). When North Italians cook fresh cod in a leek-tomato sauce and serve it with polenta, they drink red wine. The Spanish Basques insist on red wine with their many salt-dried-cod creations. Lamprey, as done in Bordeaux, calls for red wine in the sauce and more of the same to drink. Many of these red-wine fish dishes have found their way into West Coast fish cookery.

The West has come up with some of her own—crab cioppino, barbecued salmon, ling cod baked with a mayonnaise mask.

In the West, one fact is immutable: Red wine is fishermen's wine. And that makes a strong case for it. Everywhere you go up and down the West Coast, the fishermen testify to the virtues of the so-called lowly fish, the trash fish—the anchovies and mackerel, the squid and yellowtail and cod. These fish tend to be the full-flavored fish. And the fishermen's red wine balances them. Likewise, the fishermen invented crab cioppino; and red wine is cioppino wine.

The red wines with fish are often chilled red wines—chilled for more refreshment and chilled for a mellower taste. The red wines with fish are sometimes rosés.

COCONUT CRAB SOUP

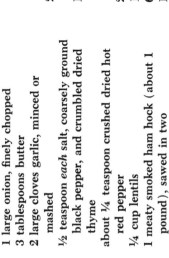

This came to California by way of the Caribbean. And it is perfectly at home, since so much of what is indigenous to the Caribbean is also local here. In re-location, the crab changed from Trini-dadian to Pacific Coast Dungeness.

Purchase coconut milk frozen, or make it yourself this way: Pour ½ cup boiling water over the grated meat of 1 coconut. Stir coconut and press down with a spoon. Allow to stand for 20 minutes. Place coconut in cheesecloth to strain; squeeze to extract all liquid.

This is a thick, full-meal soup. Bor-der each serving with lime wedges and ripe tomato wedges. Pass crisp-crusted French-style bread and butter.

1 large onion, finely chopped
3 tablespoons butter
2 large cloves garlic, minced or mashed
½ teaspoon *each* salt, coarsely ground black pepper, and crumbled dried thyme
about ¼ teaspoon crushed dried hot red pepper
¼ cup lentils
1 meaty smoked ham hock (about 1 pound), sawed in two

2 packages (10 ounces each) frozen chopped spinach
1 package (10 ounces) frozen okra, thawed slightly and coarsely chopped
2 cups water
1 cup coconut milk
6 tablespoons fresh lime juice
1 pound fresh Dungeness crab meat

In a large kettle, sauté onion in butter until limp. Stir in garlic, salt, pepper, thyme, red pepper, and lentils. Add ham hock, spinach, okra, water, coconut milk, and 4 tablespoons of the lime juice. Cover, bring to a boil, then simmer for 1½ hours, stirring occasionally. Remove ham hock; cut meat from bones and into small pieces, and return to kettle. Reserve a few crab legs for garnish. Add remaining crab to soup, along with remaining lime juice. Cook just enough to heat crab through. Taste and correct seasoning with salt and pepper if necessary. Ladle into soup plates; garnish with reserved crab legs. Makes 6 servings.

Wine suggestion: Heitz Grignolino Rosé

It takes an Italian in the Far West to tell you how to cook baccalà (Italian salt-dried cod) on a Western barbecue. Dr. Angelo Pellegrini is that Italian (and the author of The Prejudiced Palate and Wine and the Good Life). He'll also tell you there is no doubt that baccalà can take—in fact, needs—a red wine for drinking.

To prepare salt cod for grilling, soak in cold water for twenty-four to forty-eight hours, until it is very moist throughout; change water two or three times; drain well; if necessary, remove any skin and bones. Or freshen according to package directions.

BARBECUED *BACCALÀ*, ROSEMARY BASTED

½ cup olive oil
3 tablespoons wine vinegar
2 large cloves garlic, minced or mashed
several sprigs of fresh rosemary, crushed slightly to release oils
4 thick slices (about 1½ pounds) salt-dried cod prepared for grilling
additional olive oil and wine vinegar

Beat together the ½ cup olive oil, 3 tablespoons vinegar, and garlic with rosemary sprigs; let rosemary stand in mixture for 15 minutes. With rosemary, brush mixture generously over both sides of cod. Place cod on grill over medium-hot charcoal, and barbecue until heated through and somewhat smoked; turn and baste frequently. Pass cruets of additional oil and vinegar for seasoning. Makes 4 servings.

Italian descendants out of North Italy are the main seafaring and seafood-eating population around San Francisco. These Italian-backgrounded home cooks hold a glorious store of devastating ways to cook seafood. They apply their seafood savvy, passed on from Italian forefathers, to the seafood at hand in San Francisco.

One wonderful young cook who carries on the fine-food tradition of her Piedmontese ancestors—without a single modern-day cooking compromise—is Alda Maggiora. She learned her cookery from her father, who pioneered a San Francisco sausage company and who still epitomizes the Italian who lives with and loves good food.

This is Papa Maggiora's dish for a cold winter's Friday night. He still makes it—puts the cod in to soak on Wednesday, anticipating Friday night's cooking and feasting. Alda explains it:

Italian dried codfish (baccalà) is usually the flat cod with bones and skin; it takes two days to soak; then you remove bones and skin. It is easier to use the boneless, thicker pieces of dried cod. Or you can make this with fresh cod or sea bass. The frying is just to help hold the flesh together in large chunks, not for complete cooking. Papa M. adds a grated raw potato to his polenta at the beginning of his hour-long cooking and stirring—to make it much smoother. The following is a faster polenta.

COD WITH PINE NUTS AND POLENTA

golden cod (recipe opposite page)	3 tablespoons pine nuts
leek tomato sauce (opposite page)	buttered polenta (opposite page)

Break golden cod into large chunks, and arrange over bottom of a greased baking dish, about 2 quarts. Turn leek tomato sauce over fish, and sprinkle with pine nuts. Bake in a moderate oven (350°) for 25 minutes or until bubbling. To serve, spoon out a generous base of buttered polenta, and top with fish and sauce. Makes 6 servings.

Golden cod: Soak 1½ pounds thick slices of skimmed and boned dried cod (or slightly more unboned cod) in cold water until it is very moist throughout, about 24 hours; change water 2 or 3 times. (Or freshen cod according to package directions.) Drain, wipe dry, and coat lightly with flour. In a frying pan, sauté cod quickly on both sides in a generous amount of salad oil until golden.

Leek tomato sauce: Sauté 1 cup chopped leeks and ½ cup finely chopped onions in 2 tablespoons each butter and olive oil until golden. Stir in 1 large clove garlic, minced or mashed; ¾ teaspoon each salt and ground sage; ⅜ teaspoon dried thyme; and ¼ teaspoon black pepper. Add 1 large can (1 pound 12 ounces) solid-pack tomatoes and ½ cup dry white table wine. Simmer, uncovered, stirring occasionally, for 1 hour or until well blended. Stir in 4 tablespoons chopped fresh parsley.

Buttered polenta: Stirring constantly with a wire whisk, gradually add 1 cup polenta or yellow cornmeal and 1 teaspoon salt to 4 cups boiling water. Cook, stirring, for 5 minutes. Stir in 3 tablespoons butter. Turn into a buttered baking dish, about 1½ quarts. Bake in a moderate oven (350°) for 50 minutes or until set.

Wine suggestion: A California Chianti or Barbera

91

For the old-time fishermen who know fish so well, the lowliest fish are the best. And when you have these "lowly" fish as these fishermen cook them, you have elevated fish. These fishermen believe in the natural flavors of fish; they don't lose the fish in the spicing. For them, barbecued fresh, fresh anchovies and squid with Italian bread and red wine produce an incomparable feast.

Tod Ghio is a fish wholesaler and restaurateur in San Diego. He learned the fish business from the beginning; his father was a commercial fisherman; his mother still supervises—and often cooks—in the famed Anthony's seafood restaurants in the San Diego area.

Ghio still likes to cook the simple way "out back on a fish box." Occasionally he stokes up a little hibachi out in back of his harbor office and calls the head of the fish and game department and a few others who know good fish to eat this fish dish—and sourdough bread, green salad, and red wine.

This marinating-basting sauce is Ghio's upgrading of the old-time Italian fisherman's "stern-of-the-boat" sauce of olive oil, rosemary, and parsley. He says there's no doubt but what you drink red wine with this fish; "The fishermen drank red wine with it."

Use this on fillets of any of the so-called trash fish—bonita, yellowtail, barracuda, mackerel. He favors mackerel—either the Pacific mackerel, also called blue or American, or the Jack mackerel, sometimes called Spanish.

PARSLEY-BARBECUED MACKEREL

3 pounds mackerel fillets
Ghio's sauce epicurean (recipe below)

Marinate mackerel in sauce epicurean for 2 hours. Barbecue fillets on greased grill over moderate coals, turning twice and basting frequently with marinade, until fish flakes with a fork. Makes 6 servings.

Ghio's sauce epicurean: Shake or beat together ½ cup each olive oil and salad oil, ⅓ cup each dry white wine and white wine vinegar, ¼ cup finely chopped parsley, 2 tablespoons catsup, 1 tablespoon salt, 1 teaspoon crumbled dried rosemary, and ⅛ teaspoon black pepper.

WINE POACHED SABLEFISH AND POTATOES

1 whole sablefish (also called
    black cod or butterfish), about
    4 pounds, cleaned, or about 3
    pounds sablefish fillets or steaks

wine court bouillon (recipe below)
4 medium-size potatoes, sliced
    chopped fresh parsley
    caper butter (below)

Wrap fish in cheesecloth and lower into kettle of simmering court bouillon. (If necessary, add more boiling water so liquid just covers fish.) Add potatoes to kettle. Cover and simmer until fish flakes with a fork, about 30 minutes for whole fish, about 15 minutes for fillets. Lift fish from kettle, drain, unwrap, and place on warm serving platter. (If necessary, quickly cook potatoes further until tender; drain.) Arrange potatoes alongside fish. Sprinkle with parsley. Pass caper butter. Makes 6 servings.

Wine court bouillon: Combine in a large kettle 2 quarts water; 1 cup dry white wine; 3 large parsley sprigs; 1 onion, sliced; juice and rind of 1 lemon; 2 large peeled cloves garlic; 1 tablespoon salt; and ½ teaspoon whole black peppercorns. Cover and simmer for 20 minutes.

Caper butter: Combine 1 cup melted butter and 1½ tablespoons capers and heat through.

Wine suggestion: A California Chianti

The sablefish flesh is so rich and sumptuous just in itself that it needs no saucing; and it commands red wine for drinking. But, if you wish, ladle a little of the caper butter over the fish as well as the potatoes.

For Portuguese fishermen in Portugal and in California, wine is red. Two of their dishes bear witness to the suitability of red wine with fish. Squeeze lemon juice over as you eat.

95

PORTUGUESE PORK AND CLAMS

2 pounds boneless pork butt,
    cut into 1-inch cubes
4 teaspoons paprika
salt and freshly ground black pepper
4 large cloves garlic,
    minced or mashed
2 whole bay leaves
1½ cups dry white wine
2 pounds small steaming clams
about 3 tablespoons lard

2 medium-size onions, very thinly
    sliced
1 jar or can (4 ounces)
    sliced pimentos
few drops liquid hot-pepper seasoning
hot boiled new potatoes
lemon wedges
chopped fresh parsley and/or
    chopped fresh coriander

Mix pork, paprika, 1 teaspoon salt, ½ teaspoon pepper, garlic, bay, and wine; cover and chill for 12 hours (or marinate at room temperature for about 3 hours). Scrub clams well, soak in cold water for 1 hour, drain, and rinse. Drain pork well, saving marinade. In a large frying pan or kettle with cover, brown pork well over medium heat in about 1 tablespoon lard. Add marinade and cook, uncovered, until liquid is almost completely reduced. Turn out of pan. Melt remaining lard in frying pan, add onions, and sauté until limp. Return pork mixture to pan along with pimentos, liquid hot-pepper seasoning, and clams. Cover and cook over low heat for 15 minutes or until clams open. Stir gently to mix; taste and correct seasoning. Serve onto warm rimmed serving plates or platter, bordered with potatoes and lemon wedges. Sprinkle generously with parsley and coriander. Makes 4 generous servings.

Wine suggestion: A California Grignolino

ESCABECHE À PORTUGUESA

This is meant for a supper: Chilled vinaigrette-marinated fish with hot roasted potatoes in their skins, and plenty of red wine. Almost any smooth-tasting popularly priced red wine will do.

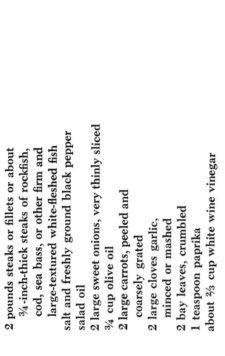

2 pounds steaks or fillets or about ¾-inch-thick steaks of rockfish, cod, sea bass, or other firm and large-textured white-fleshed fish
salt and freshly ground black pepper
salad oil
2 large sweet onions, very thinly sliced
¾ cup olive oil
2 large carrots, peeled and coarsely grated
2 large cloves garlic, minced or mashed
2 bay leaves, crumbled
1 teaspoon paprika
about ⅔ cup white wine vinegar

Season fish with salt and pepper. Quickly fry in a generous amount of salad oil until flesh flakes with a fork. Let cool; remove any skin and bones; break into large chunks. In a large frying pan, sauté onions in olive oil until limp. Stir in carrots, garlic, bay, about 1½ teaspoons salt, about ¼ teaspoon pepper, paprika, and vinegar. Allow to cool. Arrange fish and onion mixture in alternate layers in earthenware or glass deep bowl or wide-mouthed jar. Cover and chill for 2 days (longer is better), up to 3 weeks. Makes about 6 servings.

In this almond-abundant West, the Greeks don't have to rely on mashed potatoes or bread crumbs or any other ingredients for the thickening media of their Skordalia; they can make it totally rich of toasted ground almonds—and garlic and lemon and oil. They melt this cloaking and seasoning sauce into fish and accompanying eggplant, both fried or broiled or charcoal-broiled crisp and golden brown. Use any firm-textured white fish such as cod, bass, swordfish, or rockfish.

This most magnificent of the Skordalias is the recipe of California Food Consultant Lou Pappas.

TOASTED ALMOND SKORDALIA

2 egg yolks
2 tablespoons white wine vinegar
1 tablespoon fresh lemon juice
4 large cloves garlic, minced or mashed
1 teaspoon salt
1 cup olive oil
½ cup finely ground blanched almonds, lightly toasted

Put egg yolks, vinegar, lemon juice, garlic, and salt in blender container; whirl to blend. Turn blender on low speed and gradually pour in oil in a fine, steady stream through opening in container top; blend until smooth. Stir in almonds. Makes about 1¾ cups sauce, enough for 6 to 8 servings of fish and eggplant.

Note: To toast almonds, sprinkle on baking sheet, and lightly brown in a moderate oven (350°); stir or shake occasionally.

ITALIAN ANCHOVIES ON SKEWER

Thread several whole cleaned anchovies on a thin bamboo skewer, spearing each fish through the center, just below the bone. Place on greased grill over moderately hot coals with "bellies up, bones on bottom. Keep the flesh part of the fish up at first." Turn once (and the bone holds the fish on skewer). Grill until fish flakes. During grilling, baste frequently with lemon-tomato baste (recipe below). When ready to serve, slide off skewer. "Eat one side like a harmonica. Then turn over and eat the other side."

Lemon-tomato baste: Beat together with a fork ½ cup salad oil; 2 tablespoons lemon juice; 3 tablespoons chopped fresh parsley; 3 tablespoons minced fresh or solid-pack canned tomatoes; 1 large clove garlic, minced or mashed; ½ teaspoon crumbled dried basil; $\frac{1}{16}$ teaspoon crumbled dried oregano; ½ teaspoon salt; and ¼ teaspoon freshly ground black pepper. Makes basting sauce for about 12 anchovies or 2 pounds salmon fillet (see page 99).

In Monterey, Italian Vince Colletto cooks for the love of it—for clubs, large group gatherings, friends with a big party on their hands. He can do anything—a steak barbecue after the golf tournament, a Maundy Thursday lamb stew for the old folks' club, a spaghetti-and-meatball dinner for the yacht club. But his greatest renown comes with fish —a salmon barbecue, a squid dinner with squid cooked seven different ways, abalone with spaghetti, lobster with spaghetti. . . .

For himself, he likes nothing better than barbecued anchovies, cooked the way his father taught him. The special threading on bamboo skewers is the important part.

In the summer when the Monterey (king) salmon are in full season, the Monterey salmon barbecue becomes a way of life. At that time of year, nearly every big social event centers on the salmon barbecue. Weekend family get-togethers are salmon barbecues. Beach parties are salmon barbecues. The Monterey Salmon Barbecue doesn't call for a specific barbecuing method; every backyard or professional chef has his own convictions (everything from teriyaki to oil and lemon to an Italian garlic-tomato sauce for basting; whole, steaks, or filleted salmon); the one thing constant: fresh, fresh salmon caught that day.

Vince Colletto holds that the first thing about salmon barbecuing is to barbecue fillets, never steaks. The next thing is to barbecue by two grillings, the first to cook the fish partially so the flesh fibers open up, the second to finish cooking with the seasoning juices settling in.

Plan on a half pound of salmon fillet per person.

A MONTEREY SALMON BARBECUE

Wipe large salmon fillet pieces (skin on) with a damp cloth. Place in greased hinged broiler or on greased grill over moderate coals. Cook, turning once, until about half done (until flesh begins to feel firm when tested with fingertip, before fish flakes). Remove from heat, baste flesh generously with lemon-tomato baste (recipe on page 98), let stand for 30 minutes. Return salmon to grill, skin side down, and barbecue until heated through and fish flakes with a fork.

Wine suggestion: A California Zinfandel

BAKED STEAKS, HERB-MAYONNAISE MASKED

This fast baking is almost like a broiling; and you don't have to turn the steaks. Use this same glazing technique on thick steaks of sea bass, swordfish, or other relatively lean, large-textured, white-fleshed fish.

4 one-inch-thick lingcod steaks,
   about 2 pounds total
salt and freshly ground black pepper
1 cup mayonnaise
3 tablespoons sour cream
1 tablespoon olive oil
1½ teaspoons fresh lemon juice
1 teaspoon white wine vinegar
2 teaspoons crumbled dried tarragon
4 teaspoons *each* snipped fresh
   chives and chopped fresh parsley
1 teaspoon dried dill weed
½ teaspoon celery salt

Wipe fish with a damp cloth. Season generously on both sides with salt and pepper. Place on a greased shallow baking tray. Mix remaining ingredients and spoon over fish surfaces. Bake in a very hot oven (450°) for 15 minutes or just until fish flakes. Makes 4 servings.

Wine suggestion: With lingcod—a dry rosé; with sea bass, cod, or swordfish—a light-bodied red wine, slightly chilled

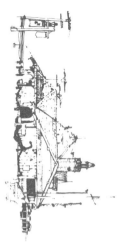

CHAPTER 7

OF RESTAURANT RENOWN

Western seafood eating cannot exclude restaurant eating. A fine seafood house has the know-how with seafood, the accessibility to the best, the chef's skill in cooking and creating, and a menu of seafood dishes that are winners in the kitchen and on the dining table. Such houses of exquisite eating seem few. And only a sampling of these are honored in the recipes here.

Besides these extraordinary restaurants, a number of other Western restaurants excel with seafood—usually because of their ability to get seafoods not available to the retail trade, or their preparation of the more complicated seafood dishes.

Otherwise, it is seldom that restaurant cookery surpasses home cooking of seafood. (A well-intended comment about the cookery at one fish restaurant was: "They put it in a pan and swear it done." The tasting proved the prediction.) Most home cooks can apply what best exalts most seafood: an uncomplicated approach to superior ingredients.

Hopefully, you can have the best of both restaurant know-how and home-kitchen execution in the following sampling—a few of the outstanding Western restaurant recipes adapted to preparing at home.

Vic Bergeron, alias Restaurateur Trader Vic, is a power in the Western food and wine world—and deservingly so. He is an innovator and a pacesetter but always on the highest level. He knows food and drink, and he knows the West and Western people. He believes in a West Coast cuisine that is suited to our time and tempo of life—and our natural products. Yet he is not against imported products; he believes they are a part of today's Western living just as much as are Western indigenous food products. He views Western people with this pro-nouncement: Our people just love to dress in an interesting manner; and they dance and enjoy art and music when it is likewise interesting. And the same thing goes for food. They'll experiment with anything. They're not conformists.

From his executive office in the San Francisco Trader Vic restaurant, Trader Vic told the story behind his renowned Bongo Bongo Soup. It is one story of how great recipes begin: out of need.

Traveling in New Zealand before the second World War, the Trader tasted a New Zealander's bisque of the local tohoroa clam—small, tender clams that feed on green algae. He was so impressed by that soup that he began importing the tohoroa clams to his restaurants, making the soup, and establishing it on menus as Bongo Bongo Soup. Then the war came, and the New Zealand clams were not available. The soup was too popular to banish. So the ingenious Trader devised another one, nearly the same, of products that were available—oysters and spinach.

It has been called a "fantastic cream of puréed oysters."

TRADER VIC'S BONGO BONGO SOUP

2½ cups half and half (half milk, half cream)
10 ounces fresh oysters, poached and whirled in blender to purée, or 1 can (9½ ounces) oyster purée
¼ cup puréed cooked spinach or strained creamed spinach baby food
2 tablespoons butter
1½ teaspoons monosodium glutamate
1 teaspoon A.1. sauce
about ½ teaspoon salt
about ⅜ teaspoon freshly ground black pepper
generous dash of garlic salt
generous dash of cayenne
2 teaspoons cornstarch mixed with 2 teaspoons cold water
about ⅔ cup heavy cream, whipped

In a large saucepan, heat half and half just to simmering. Add oyster purée, spinach, butter, monosodium glutamate, A.1. sauce, salt, pepper, garlic salt, and cayenne. Heat to simmering, stirring with a whisk until smooth; do not boil. Add cornstarch mixture, and heat and stir with a whisk until soup is slightly thickened. Correct seasoning with salt and pepper. Ladle soup into heat-proof serving bowls. Top each with a spoonful of whipped cream. Slip under broiler (about 5 inches from heat) just until cream is well glazed with brown. Serve immediately. Makes 8 first-course servings.

for the rest of my days if Jack's did the cooking." This praise has been echoed by nearly every other eater who has partaken of the dish.

Each serving is two folded fillets of sole in a silver platter, smothered with a devastating crab-and-shrimp sauce, and glazed to a lacy brown over the top. The sauce is at the breaking point of richness, absolutely too rich for sanity, and marvelous.

There is not, properly, a place in this book for the French seafood classics. But there is a place for Sole Marguery as they do it at Jack's. It has become a California classic.

To be unrivaled seems an unlikely state, but Jack's Sole Marguery seems to have made it. Doris Muscatine, in A Cook's Tour of San Francisco, raved about it as "A dish I could eat happily

JACK'S SOLE MARGUERY

8 small sole fillets
(about 2 pounds total)
salt and pepper
3 tablespoons minced shallots
1/4 pound fresh mushrooms,
thinly sliced
12 Dungeness crab legs (about
4 ounces)

3 ounces tiny shrimp
1 cup dry white wine
1 cup fish stock or water
1 cup heavy (whipping) cream
4 tablespoons Hollandaise sauce
(recipe below)

Season sole fillets lightly with salt and pepper, and fold each in half, crosswise. Arrange in a single layer in a buttered baking dish (or broiling-serving platter). Sprinkle with shallots, mushrooms, crab, and shrimp. Add wine and stock. Bake in a moderate oven (350°) for about 15 minutes or until fish flakes with a fork. Carefully remove sole, mushrooms, crab, and shrimp to a buttered broiling-serving platter (or pour off juices into a saucepan). Add cream to baking juices and cook over high heat, stirring, until reduced to a thick sauce. Remove from heat and stir in Hollandaise. Pour sauce over sole and slip under broiler (about 6 inches from heat) until glazed with brown. Makes 4 servings.

Hollandaise sauce: Put 3 egg yolks, 2 tablespoons fresh lemon juice, 1/4 teaspoon salt, and a pinch of cayenne in blender container. Heat 1/2 cup butter until it bubbles; do not brown. Turn blender on high speed, and immediately pour in hot butter in a steady stream through small opening in blender cover. Add 1/2 teaspoon Dijon-style mustard, and whirl until blended, about 15 seconds. Makes 3/4 to 1 cup sauce. Note: To reheat remaining sauce for later use, place in top part of double boiler over hot (not boiling) water; stir until smooth and warm.

Wine suggestion: Souverain White Pinot

To be completely honest about it, San Francisco is a seafood eater's paradise as much for her gathering-in of the choicest seafood from all over the world as for the fish and shellfish from her own waters. One Bay Area fish man counts it a prime location because "We've got it coming from every place in the world—the best from Europe and the Orient and the southern seas, and the wonderful local fish."

One of those prize imports provides the possibility of a sublime Indian delicacy served at the Taj of India Restaurant. The item: giant prawns from the Cochin Sea off India's south coast. Prepared under the guidance and inspiration of Restaurateur Sushil Kakar, these plumply meated prawns are marinated in an exotic sesame sauce, charcoal-grilled in their shells, and served with a spicing sauce to ladle over the prawns as you eat.

Since the magnificent Cochin prawns are not available in consumer markets, Mr. Kakar suggests using spiny lobster tails at home. Or, if you can get prawns as large as two to four ounces each, use them: Gently loosen meat from shell by inserting a thin-bladed dull knife between meat and shell. With a small sharp knife, cut meat at the back of the shell and remove vein, being careful to keep shell intact. Insert marinade as for lobster tails. (Do not remove or cut the underside of the shell.) Grill over charcoal until peach-colored, firm, and opaque, about 12 minutes; or bake in a very hot oven (450°) for about 10 minutes, turning once.

The sesame oil should be the light, straw-colored kind. When using a sesame oil that is heavier and darker, dilute with half light salad oil.

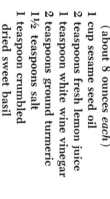

SESAME LOBSTER (OR PRAWNS), MOGUL STYLE

4 spiny lobster tails
  (about 8 ounces *each*)
1 cup sesame seed oil
2 teaspoons fresh lemon juice
1 teaspoon white wine vinegar
2 teaspoons ground turmeric
1½ teaspoons salt
1 teaspoon crumbled
  dried sweet basil

½ teaspoon crumbled dried mint
  about ½ teaspoon *each*
  crushed dried red peppers and
  coarsely ground black pepper
⅛ teaspoon ground coriander
  romaine leaves and lemon slices for
  garnish

Thaw frozen lobster tails. Cut away and remove under shells. Cut each in half lengthwise, through shell. With a thin-bladed dull knife, partially loosen lobster meat from shell. Make a cut down center of lobster meat, cutting about halfway to shell. Shake or beat together oil and remaining ingredients except romaine and lemon slices to make marinade. Spoon as much marinade as possible into crevice between lobster meat and shell; spoon more marinade over top of flesh and into center groove. Let stand for 1 hour. Place lobster on grill over moderately hot coals and barbecue, turning once or twice and basting flesh side with marinade, for about 10 minutes or until meat loses translucence. (Or lay tails flat, shell side down, on broiler pan; broil about 5 inches from heat for about 7 minutes.) Arrange tails on plates lined with romaine and garnished with lemon slices. Heat remaining marinade just to warm; serve in a small bowl with ladle, and pass. Makes 4 servings.

In San Francisco, one of the best Chinese restaurants is not in Chinatown but on Polk Street. It serves not the usual Cantonese cuisine but North Chinese. The policy at The Mandarin is to avoid a great adapting to American tastes; rather, it is to keep North Chinese dishes as close as possible to the original.

According to The Mandarin owner, Mrs. Sun Yung Chiang, North China is generally meat-eating territory, except for its one famous dish of sweet and sour fish. (The Cantonese also produce sweet and sour fish, but their technique is a copy of the North China way; the Cantonese excel, rather, in their steaming of fish.)

The Mandarin sweet and sour sauce is the restaurant's own, and typical of the North China sauce. It is not like the too common, too fruit-sweet, too slick sweet and sour sauces.

Two fryings is the secret of this dish.

It is important that the fish be completely cooled after the first frying before the second; then the skin takes on its lovely bronze color and crispness.

At The Mandarin, the presentation is spectacular: The whole fish is perched, standing up straight in an oval platter, cloaked in the deep red sauce, and with colorful slivers of carrot, green pepper, and celery cascading over. A parsley sprig sits like a crown on the fish's head. To serve, you break the thick layers of fish flesh away from the bone.

SWEET AND SOUR FISH, THE MANDARIN

1 whole rockfish (rock cod),
   carp, or red snapper,
   about 2½ pounds
1 egg
2 tablespoons *each* soy sauce and
   dry sherry
2 teaspoons grated or very finely
   minced fresh ginger
1 teaspoon salt

about ½ teaspoon freshly ground
   black pepper
cornstarch
salad oil
sweet and sour sauce (recipe below)
slivers of green bell peppers
   and carrots
thin diagonal slivers of celery
Chinese parsley (fresh coriander)
   sprigs

Clean fish well, leaving head, tail, and fins intact. With a sharp knife, score fish flesh on each side with about 6 parallel deep slashes. Beat together the egg, soy, sherry, ginger, salt, and pepper; rub over surface of fish and deep into scoring lines. Coat fish with cornstarch, and rub into scoring lines. Heat about ½ inch salad oil over moderately high heat in frying pan (to about 375°). Add fish, and brown well on one side; turn and brown on second side, about 8 minutes total. Place fish on a rack to cool thoroughly. Shortly before serving, return fish to hot oil and fry on both sides until crisp, about 4 minutes total. Remove to warm serving platter. Pour hot sweet and sour sauce over fish. Sprinkle generously with green-pepper, carrot, and celery slivers. Surround with parsley. Makes 2 servings.

Sweet and sour sauce: Combine in saucepan ¾ cup water; ¼ cup each sugar, catsup, and soy sauce; and 2 tablespoons wine vinegar; heat to bubbling. Mix 2 tablespoons cornstarch and ¼ cup cold water and gradually add to saucepan, stirring. Continue to cook and stir over medium heat until sauce is smooth and thickened.

WHIPPED HORSERADISH CREAM

1 cup heavy (whipping) cream
about 2 tablespoons prepared
   horseradish
2 teaspoons fresh lemon juice
1 teaspoon sugar
generous grinding of black pepper

Whip cream, and fold in remaining ingredients. Spoon into serving bowl, and chill for at least 1 hour. Makes about 2 cups.

An eating landmark in Portland is the London Grill of the Benson Hotel. One of the most delicious appetizers there is the glorious local Columbia River salmon with sweet onion and sweet cream. Chef Ivan Runge has designed it to be carved and served at your table.

They present a handsome, great fillet slab of moist smoked salmon. The waiter carves tissue-thin slices of it, and lifts them onto soft leaves of lettuce. Each plate serving is bordered with fine rings of sweet onions and garnished with stuffed olives and capers. Accompaniments are thin slices of buttered rye melba toast and a horseradish and whipped-cream sauce to be the luxury finish over the salmon.

A Western Pan Roast used to get a North Italian treatment at the hands of the late Joseph Bona, owner and executive chef of the Vila d'Este on the San Francisco Peninsula.

Chef Bona chose Eastern bluepoints for the oysters, but you can use Pacific oysters. He served a wonderfully scented risotto on the side—suggestive of saffron, a lot of golden browned butter, and fresh lemon. The juices of the pan roast mingle with the rice.

OYSTERS PEPEROTTE, VILA D'ESTE

about 4 tablespoons butter
¼ pound fresh mushrooms,
   thinly sliced
1 green bell pepper, cut into very
   thin slivers about 1½ inches long
3 tablespoons minced shallots
1 jar (10 or 12 ounces) Eastern
   bluepoint oysters (or Pacific
   oysters cut into two
   or three pieces), drained

salt and freshly ground
   black pepper
dash of liquid hot-pepper seasoning
¼ cup dry white table wine
   or dry vermouth
2 tablespoons diced canned pimentos
   parsley, chopped and sprigs

Melt 2 tablespoons of the butter in a large frying pan. Add mushrooms, and sauté until coated with butter and tender; push to edge of pan. Add 1 more tablespoon of the butter and the green pepper; sauté just until limp. Stir in shallots; push peppers and shallots to side of pan. Melt remaining tablespoon butter in frying pan, add oysters, and sauté over low heat for about 3 minutes; turn; sprinkle generously with salt and pepper to season, liquid hot-pepper seasoning, wine, and pimentos. Continue cooking just until oyster edges curl and wine cooks down slightly, about 3 minutes. Gently mix all ingredients in pan and serve onto warm plates. Sprinkle with chopped parsley; garnish with parsley sprigs. Makes 2 servings.

BEEFSTEAK NEPTUNE, FIVE CROWNS

The Los Angeles area doesn't abound in great seafood-eating restaurants. A few places do a few nice things. One is Restaurant Five Crowns at Corona del Mar. In an Old English atmosphere, you can get this very Western specialty. It is the creation of Hans Prager, executive chef for Lawry's restaurants. The creation happened thanks to Chef Prager's enthusiasm for Western Dungeness crab. Prager has traveled the waters of the world tasting their seafood; and, from our Western waters, he considers Dungeness crab the topmost delight.

His Beefsteak Neptune is his Western embellishment of classic Veal Oscar: Instead of veal cutlets, he uses butterflied fillet of beef; instead of lobster, Western Dungeness; instead of Hollandaise, Béarnaise.

He suggests French fried potatoes on the side. He suggests a tart rosé for the wine—not as a compromise between meat and seafood, but as the wine that simply tastes right with this dish.

fillet of beef butterflied to
    1-inch thickness (about 10 ounces)
about ½ tablespoon butter
salt and pepper
4 spears hot cooked fresh asparagus
4 or 5 Dungeness crab legs
about 2 tablespoons Béarnaise
    sauce (recipe below)

In a frying pan, sauté steak in butter until cooked to doneness you desire (about 4 minutes each side over medium-high heat for rare). Season lightly with salt and pepper, and place on warm serving plate. Top with asparagus, then crab legs; spoon a ribbon of Béarnaise over the top. Makes 1 serving.

Béarnaise sauce: Combine in a small pan 2 teaspoons minced shallots (or green onions), ¼ teaspoon freshly ground black pepper, 2 tablespoons dry white wine, and 1 tablespoon wine vinegar; cook rapidly until liquid is absorbed. Put in blender container 3 egg yolks, 2 tablespoons fresh lemon juice, 1½ teaspoons crumbled dried tarragon, ¼ teaspoon salt, and a pinch of cayenne. Heat ½ cup butter until it bubbles; do not brown. Turn blender on high speed and immediately pour in hot butter in a steady stream through small opening in blender cover. Add shallot mixture and whirl until blended, about 30 seconds. Makes ¾ to 1 cup sauce.
Note: To reheat remaining sauce for later use, place in top part of double boiler over hot (not boiling) water; stir until smooth and warm.

The sauce is the secret of the excellent barbecued swordfish and butterflied shrimp at the Lobster House in Santa Barbara. And localities know it; they often buy the sauce and the seafood at the Lobster House and take them both home for barbecuing.

BARBECUED SWORDFISH, LOBSTER HOUSE

1 cup tomato catsup
½ cup salad oil
2 tablespoons Worcestershire sauce
2 large cloves garlic, minced or mashed
1½ teaspoons crumbled dried rosemary
1 bay leaf, crumbled
1½ teaspoons salt
1 teaspoon coarsely ground black pepper
about 3 pounds ¾-inch-thick swordfish steaks

Beat together with a fork all ingredients except swordfish; pour over fish. Marinate at room temperature for 30 minutes or more; turn fish once or twice. Remove fish from marinade, place on oiled grill over moderately hot charcoal, and grill for about 10 minutes total or just until fish flakes with a fork; turn fish and baste with marinade frequently. Makes 6 to 8 servings.

AVOCADO CRAB CRÊPES, IMPERIAL DYNASTY

A most amazing thing: to find in the tiny town of Hanford, lost in the middle of California's vast San Joaquin Valley farming lands, the smart Restaurant Imperial Dynasty. More amazing: the regal seafood offerings in this inland-town setting. The reason: Chef Richard C. Wing.

Chef Wing says you can substitute minced cooked shrimp meat or flaked fresh or canned salmon for the crab. Regardless, the effect is merciless rich-ness. You have to be willing to take some time to do this.

avocado-crab filling (recipe opposite page)
12 crêpes (opposite page)
curry sauce (opposite page)
avocado slices dipped in lemon juice, mandarin orange sections, and lime wedges for garnish

Spread one twelfth of the avocado filling over center of each crêpe and roll up, folding in ends if you wish. Place two filled crêpes in each of 6 individual buttered baking-serving platters, or place filled crêpes side by side in a shallow buttered baking platter. Spoon curry sauce over crêpes. Bake in a moderate oven (350°) for 12 minutes or until heated through. Garnish with avocado slices, mandarin oranges, and lime wedges. Makes 6 servings.

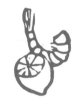

Avocado-crab filling: Peel 4 large ripe avocados, remove seeds, and mash until nearly smooth. Add 2 cups (about 1 pound) flaked crab meat, 1 tablespoon minced green onions, 1 tablespoon finely chopped Chinese parsley (fresh coriander), 1 tablespoon fresh lime juice, 1 tablespoon brandy, 1 tablespoon Dijon-style mustard, about 1 teaspoon curry powder, and 1 slightly beaten egg white. Mix thoroughly until creamy. Add salt and black pepper to season well.

Crêpes: Beat 4 eggs slightly. Add ½ cup flour and ½ teaspoon salt, and beat until smooth. Gradually add 1⅓ cups milk, beating until batter is smooth. Heat butter (about ½ teaspoon for each crêpe) over medium-high heat in a 7- or 8-inch crêpe pan. Pour in about 3 tablespoons batter; quickly tilt and rotate pan so batter covers bottom. When lightly brown on bottom, turn and brown on second side. Slip onto a clean towel. Makes at least 12 crêpes.

Curry sauce: In a frying pan or saucepan, sauté 2 small onions, minced; ½ large apple, peeled and minced; and 1 small clove garlic, minced or mashed, in 3 tablespoons butter over medium heat for about 3 minutes; stir occasionally. Add about 1 tablespoon curry powder, and cook and stir for 2 minutes more. Stir in 3 tablespoons flour to make a paste. Gradually add 2 cups well-seasoned chicken stock; cook over low heat, stirring occasionally, until sauce is thickened, smooth, and blended, about 15 minutes. Stir in ½ cup heavy (whipping) cream, 2 teaspoons Dijon-style mustard, 1 tablespoon finely chopped mango chutney, 1 tablespoon crushed pineapple, 1 tablespoon brandy, 1 teaspoon fresh lemon juice, and, if necessary, salt and pepper to season.

CHAPTER 8

PROVINCIAL PASSIONS

These are the strictly local seafoods and seafood dishes. If you travel in the West, try to taste them. If you live in the West, cook them in their regions.

This chapter tells of some Western seafood eating that is outstanding because it is of special seafood from a special Western place. Most of these provincial pleasures are the really simple cooking treatments that rely heavily, almost totally, on the particular fresh fish. It takes a particular seafood to bring these dishes to their ultimate, and only their execution with local fish can do them justice.

But it is not just the local seafood catch that accounts for regional differences. It is also the local people. Up north, for example, the fishermen are often Nordics and not of the same temper as the Mediterraneans you find fishing along the California coastline. And each group in each area approaches the cooking of fish in its own special way.

In addition to the fish pointed out in the recipes following, Dungeness crab and, obviously, whatever local fish is freshly caught, here are some suggestions of special local tastes to seek out:

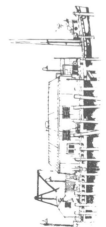

PACIFIC OCEAN

ALASKA

BRITISH COLUMBIA

Olympia Seattle
Westport
Astoria
Portland Columbia River

WASHINGTON

OREGON

Crescent City
Humboldt Bay

Eureka

Sacramento River
Placerville
Berkeley
Oakland

Point Arena
Tomales Bay
San Francisco

Santa Cruz
Monterey
Morro Bay
Santa Barbara
Los Angeles San Pedro
San Diego

Fresno

CALIFORNIA

MEXICO

Smoked sablefish (black cod). Seattle area. Also called smoked Alaska cod.

Halibut cheeks. Seattle and Portland areas. During halibut season, generally April through August.

Salmon cheeks. Seattle and Portland areas. During salmon season, generally May through September.

Olympia oysters. Seattle area. West's only native oyster. Very small, very delicate, very expensive. Eat raw with lemon juice and possibly black pepper.

Rex sole. San Francisco and area. Order it sautéed *meunière*. Have the waiter bone it for you—before you. ("When it's cooked with the bone, it keeps the flavor.")

California pompano. Monterey. Related to Eastern butterfish; about six inches long, flat, silvery, delicate. Available irregularly throughout the year.

Spiny lobster. Santa Barbara to Mexico. Have it broiled. Season mid-October to mid-March.

Swordfish. Santa Barbara to Mexico. Best July to October.

Sculpin. San Diego area. One of the choicest of the rockfish family, with meaty white flesh, fine texture, mild flavor.

ST. PETERSBURG SHRIMP CANAPÉ

Alaska shrimp are local shrimp to Seattle residents. So a Seattle hostess designates the tiny pink St. Petersburg shrimp for this canapé.

But you can use any of the tiny ocean shrimp from anywhere along the Pacific Coast. (Eureka has big landings; from about May to November you can visit commercial fishing houses along the wharf and see large rooms full of great piles of miniature pink shrimp, with bandanaed women peeling them, one by one, to get a one-inch arc of sweet meat.)

about 1 large sweet onion, cut (top to bottom) into ¼-inch-wide wedge slices
1 pound tiny shrimp
½ cup salad oil
¼ cup wine vinegar
about 2 tablespoons prepared mustard (preferably Dijon style)
freshly ground black pepper
crackers (rye, sesame, Ritz, or wheat)

Separate onion wedges into small arcs; combine with shrimp. Beat oil, vinegar, mustard, and a generous grinding of pepper together with a rotary beater until smooth and thickened; pour over shrimp and onions. Cover and chill for 12 hours or more; turn occasionally. Turn into serving bowl and surround with crackers. To serve, fork a few shrimp and onions onto a cracker. Makes appetizers for 8 to 12.

118

Tradition in the West is to serve salad first, as a first course. When and where the tiny whitebait (miniature true smelt, three to five inches long) are fresh (mostly in the summertime, anywhere along the Coast), they're fried crisp and served with the salad almost like crackers. They are so tiny, you can pick them up in your fingers and eat them bone, tail, and all.

WHITEBAIT WITH THE SALAD

Plan on about 1 pound whitebait to accompany 6 first-course green salads. To clean, break off head of each fish and pull it off with the vein. Rinse fish and dry with cloth or paper towels. Beat 1 egg slightly with 1 tablespoon milk. Dip each fish into egg mixture, then roll in cracker meal to coat. Heat about ⅛ inch salad oil in frying pan over moderately high heat. Place fish in pan without crowding and cook quickly until golden brown on one side; turn carefully and brown on the other. Remove from pan and drain on paper towels. Sprinkle generously with salt and pepper. Serve hot.

OLD-TIMERS' SWEDISH CRAYFISH

4 quarts water
1 large onion, sliced
1 large carrot, sliced
3 large cloves garlic, peeled and split
4 tablespoons salt
2 tablespoons whole pickling spice
about 8 sprigs fresh dill or 2 tablespoons dried dill weed
2 quarts cleaned live crayfish
melted butter (optional)

Combine all ingredients except crayfish and butter in a kettle and bring to a boil. Add crayfish, cover, return liquid to boiling, and boil for 6 minutes. Remove kettle from heat. Let crayfish cool in liquid or serve as soon as cool enough to handle, with melted butter for dipping. Makes about 4 snack or first-course servings with beer.

No less an authority than Jake, of Jake's Crawfish House in Portland, says, "Beer always with crayfish; crayfish aren't good without beer." (Whether it's the beer or the crayfish, the local story is that "people come from all over hell to eat crayfish at Jake's.")

All summer long, the crayfish are in Washington, Oregon, and northern California rivers and lakes and streams, and available just for the fishing.

A crayfishing expedition is a favorite summer custom for many families, especially those of Swedish descent, who seem to have an innate taste for dill-boiled crayfish and beer, just as their Swedish ancestors did.

Gathering butter (Washington) clams is popular sport in the mud flats of the bays all along the coast. Most people steam them. But on the little Italian fishing boat Panther, off Seattle, they handle the big ones this way. It is a simultaneous frying and steaming.

CLAMS PANTHER

With a strong, thin-bladed knife, cut each large butter clam in half, between shells, slicing meat in two. Heat a lot of olive oil in a frying pan. Add a lot of finely chopped onions, and sauté until limp. Turn clam halves upside-down (shell side up) in frying pan, and fry until meat and onions are golden. Turn right side up, spoon onions over meat, and use the clam shell as the clam dish. Season with salt and pepper.

HALIBUT ON A BED OF FENNEL

4 cups sliced green onions with part
   of green tops
olive oil
3 to 4 tablespoons finely chopped fresh
   fennel leaves
2 pounds halibut fillet
salt and freshly ground black pepper
1 large lemon, very thinly sliced

Sauté onions in about 4 tablespoons olive oil until limp. Spread over bottom of baking-serving platter in an area slightly larger than halibut piece. Sprinkle with fennel. Wipe halibut with a damp cloth, and season generously on both sides with salt and pepper. Place on onions; brush generously with olive oil; cover with lemon slices. Bake in a moderate oven (350°) until fish flakes with a fork, about 20 minutes. Makes 4 servings.

You have to be ultra-alert to both the halibut and the fennel season to get them both together when they are fresh. The fresh fennel season extends just through March; the fresh Pacific halibut season begins at the end of March. Traditionally this is a Greek dish, special for the week before Easter, and that is about the time that you can manage this short-term juxtaposition of ingredients. (New spring green onions, the "piles of 'em" called for, are good and abundant then, too.)

If you miss the fennel season, you can come close to the same fresh-fennel sensation by substituting about one tablespoon of fennel seeds for the snipped fresh fennel leaves.

Astoria, Oregon, is in the heart of the Northwest salmon country; it is renowned the world over for its Columbia River salmon.

The Finns around Astoria make up the majority of the local salmon fishermen; and their old-country ways come into the cooking of it.

So it is appropriate that in 1958, in a local "Savory Seafoods Search" recipe competition, a Finnish fisherman's wife won with a traditional Finnish salmon dish.

ASTORIA LAKSLODA

1 pound smoked salmon (or salt salmon), thinly sliced
4 medium-size potatoes, peeled and cut into slices ⅛ to ¼ inch thick
1 medium-size onion, finely chopped
freshly ground black pepper (optional)
1 tablespoon flour
16 whole allspice
1 large can (about 14 ounces) evaporated milk
¾ cup water
3 tablespoons melted butter
2 tablespoons butter
chopped fresh parsley

Soak salt salmon in cold water overnight; rinse and drain well. Do not soak smoked salmon. Arrange potatoes, onions, salmon, and pepper to taste in alternate layers in a buttered 2-quart casserole, beginning and ending with potatoes; when half the ingredients are layered, sprinkle surface with flour, then continue layering. Sprinkle with allspice. Mix milk, water, and melted butter, and pour over casserole contents. (If necessary, add a little more water so ingredients are just covered.) Dot with butter. Bake in a slow oven (325°) for 1 hour or until potatoes are tender. Sprinkle with parsley. Makes 6 to 8 servings.

Generally, in the Northwest, the Norwegians are the halibut fishermen and the Slavs and Scandinavians are the salmon fishermen.

In the community of Ballard, near the Seattle locks, there is a knot of Norwegian fishermen and their families. Community activities revolve around the fishermen's lives, and old-country customs still flourish. Every year at the spring opening of the halibut season the First Lutheran Church of Ballard holds a special service for the blessing of the halibut fleet for its upcoming dangerous days ahead. This annual event—Fishermen's Festival it is called—is a significant one, with the governor, mayor, and interested friends of the fishing industry attending. The Norwegian Male Chorus provides the music. The women's Norwegian Circle provides the refreshments in the church parlors afterward.

The wives of the halibut fishermen support their husbands in an even more organized way. They have formed the Halibut Fishermen's Wives' Association, "United to assist their men in every way to promote and protect our halibut industry." One of their forms of assistance is to encourage consumer appreciation of halibut by distributing cooking suggestions and exceptional halibut recipes.

Mrs. Art Strom is one of the most enthusiastic members of the Association, and this halibut chowder is her invention. Her chowder idea may be Northwest or New England, but her sour-cream finish is pure Norwegian.

Serve over crisp crackers, if you wish. Or serve over rye crackers and omit caraway seeds in the chowder.

GRETA STROM'S HALIBUT CHOWDER

6 slices bacon, cut into small pieces
2 medium-large onions, thinly sliced
4 cups water
3 cups ½-inch dices of raw potatoes
3 pounds skinless, boneless halibut,
   cut into about ½-inch pieces
1 large can (about 14 ounces)
   evaporated milk
2 tablespoons finely chopped
   fresh parsley
1 teaspoon caraway seeds (optional)
salt and freshly ground
   black pepper to taste
1 tablespoon melted butter
1 tablespoon flour
1 cup commercial sour cream

In a large kettle, cook bacon slowly until almost crisp. Add onions, and sauté until very tender. Add water and bring to a boil. Add potatoes and halibut. Cover and simmer until potatoes are tender, about 15 minutes. Add milk, parsley, caraway seeds, and about ¾ teaspoon salt and ¼ teaspoon pepper. Combine butter and flour to make a smooth paste; gradually add to chowder, and cook, gently stirring, until liquid is slightly thickened. Simmer for 5 minutes more. Remove from heat, gently stir in sour cream, and serve immediately. Makes 8 servings.

In fishing ports all along the coast, wherever they land fresh salmon (Westport, Astoria, Eureka, San Francisco, Monterey, etc.), the natives take pride in the summer salmon season, as if salmon were unique to their town.

In the West, we sometimes need to turn to light-colored reds and reds in order to find California wines to stand up to salmon. If you prefer white wines with salmon, you might do best by carefully chosen European whites, which tend to be more tart than California whites.

All summer long, the townspeople and university people of Seattle call upon Pete Formuzis and Roy Stevens to do their fresh salmon barbecue—for club gatherings, charitable events, 4-H round-ups. Then these two fish authorities (marketing experts for the U. S. Bureau of Commercial Fisheries) perform their famed incantations over the summer's best fresh king salmon fillets, and barbecue them to renowned lusciousness, and serve them hot with cold potato salad.

In performing their art for a crowd (barbecuing as much as eight hundred pounds of salmon), they use large metal boxes, with tops, with a grilling rack well above the wood coals so the heat is relatively low and the smoke enclosed. They use alder or apple wood for fuel.

For home-scale barbecuing, you can use a regular brazier with a hood for smoking (or fashion a hood of heavy-duty foil to enclose an open grill), and low glowing coals of apple, alder, or

126

other nonresinous wood; or charcoal briquets and smoke chips. (To use prepared smoke chips, soak chips in water for at least 30 minutes, or according to package directions. Put handfuls of chips on already glowing charcoal shortly before and occasionally during grilling.)

You can apply this treatment to fillets of any size salmon, even a part of a fillet; adjust cooking time to salmon size. Fish is done when it flakes with a fork.

SALMON BARBECUE, SEATTLE

Fillet a whole salmon, leaving skin on. Make a basting sauce of melted butter and fresh lemon juice and a very little crumbled dried oregano—about 1 cup butter, ½ cup lemon juice and ¼ teaspoon crumbled dried oregano for fillets from a 20-pound fish (Roy adds onion salt; Pete does not)—and brush over salmon flesh. Salt fish heavily and pepper generously. Let stand for 1 hour or more. Place each fillet, skin side down, on a sheet of heavy-duty aluminum foil; crimp up edges of foil to form a tray. Place on grill over low wood or charcoal-and-smoke-chip coals. Cover with hood or foil. Cook until fish flakes with a fork (about 30 to 45 minutes for fillets from a 20-pound salmon). Lift hood, baste, and check for doneness about every 5 to 10 minutes. To serve, cut flesh into serving-size pieces and lift from skin. Fillets from a 20-pound salmon make about 20 servings.

SALMON AVGOLEMENO

One way the Northwest Greeks treat Northwest salmon.

Most often a summer first course; may be a main course. Start with serving-size pieces of salmon. Serve at room temperature.

½ cup chopped fresh parsley
2 tablespoons olive oil
1½ cups water
1 teaspoon salt
¼ teaspoon freshly ground black pepper
1½ pounds skinned salmon fillets or 1-inch-thick steaks
3 egg yolks
3 tablespoons fresh lemon juice

In a frying pan, sauté parsley in olive oil just to coat with oil. Add water, salt, and pepper, and bring to a boil. Add salmon, arranging in a single layer. Reduce heat, cover, and simmer for 8 minutes or just until salmon flakes with a fork. In a small bowl, beat egg yolks until light and fluffy; slowly beat in lemon juice; gradually beat in about ¼ cup of the hot liquid from salmon. Gradually stir egg sauce into hot liquid in pan. Remove from heat, cover, and let stand for 5 minutes or until broth thickens slightly. Gently lift fish to rimmed serving platter, pour sauce over, and let cool. Makes 4 to 5 first-course servings, or 3 main-course servings.

When you have salmon in abundance, you can do such imaginative things as baking it in the summer sun. The result is a dry and different texture, and that makes a different taste.

The Greek Formuzis family in Seattle does this at least once every summer with a whole side of salmon. You can do it with any size fillet. It will work even on a warm, windy day without a lot of sun; the warm air cooks the salmon as much as the sun. The boiled greens alongside are part of the dish.

SUN-BAKED SALMON WITH SUMMER GREENS

The night before cooking, sprinkle salmon fillet with a lot of salt; keep in refrigerator. Next day, season salmon with freshly ground black pepper and a little fresh or crumbled dried oregano. Place on a rack on a tray, cover loosely with a layer of cheesecloth, and put in a warm, sunny, windy place for 3 hours or until flesh is firm and somewhat dry. Brush with olive oil and grill over charcoal (or broil in oven) until fish flakes with a fork and is heated through. Serve with hot boiled seasoned spinach or chard or other summer greens.

Along the tuna and salmon coasts, one of the most fetching summer salads is simply chunks of the chilled poached fish in a lettuce-lined salad bowl, under a cucumber sauce.

The white loin flesh of fresh tuna is almost like turkey—compact, mild, no fish taste; make sauce for it with part sour cream, part mayonnaise. Make salmon sauce with sour cream only.

Away from fresh salmon and tuna sources, make the salad of chilled canned salmon or tuna.

CUCUMBER SAUCE

½ cup peeled, seeded, and finely chopped cucumber
½ teaspoon salt
1 cup sour cream (for salmon), or ⅔ cup sour cream and ⅓ cup mayonnaise (for tuna)
2 teaspoons snipped chives
1 teaspoon finely chopped fresh dill or dried dill weed
½ teaspoon freshly ground black pepper

Sprinkle cucumbers with salt, chill for 1 hour, drain well. Add remaining ingredients, mix well, cover, and chill for 1 hour or more. Makes sauce for 3 to 4 main-dish salad servings.

Around Eureka there is an Agricultural Extension Home Advisor who has become legend for her energy and helpfulness. Along with her many other contributions, Ruth Crawford has developed, for local families and any others interested, the best ways to handle the local summer bounty of fresh tuna—how to clean, home-can, poach, broil, bake. . . . This is her broiling technique for crosswise slices of the white-meat loin of fresh tuna.

TUNA BROILED WITH BACON

fresh tuna loins, skinned and trimmed
    (or 1-inch-thick tuna steaks, skin
    removed)
bacon slices
split garlic clove (or garlic salt)
melted butter
freshly ground black pepper
seasoned salt
lemon wedges

Cut tuna loin across the grain into 1-inch-thick slices. Fit two slices together to make a large, steaklike serving. Wrap a bacon slice around each loin (or steak) serving, and secure with a toothpick. Rub both tuna surfaces with garlic. Place on foil-lined, greased, preheated broiler pan; brush surface generously with butter, and season generously with pepper and seasoned salt. Broil about 4 inches from heat for about 5 minutes each side or until fish flakes with a fork. Turn once, brushing second side with butter and seasoning. Serve with lemon wedges.

WALNUT-SCALLOPED OYSTERS

Tomales Bay, near San Francisco, is the one place in the West where oyster farmers have accomplished a successful transplant of adult Eastern oysters—to hold them alive for San Francisco markets. They are excellent for this dish, but you can also use the larger Pacific oysters (and the longer baking time).

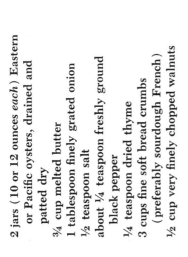

2 jars (10 or 12 ounces *each*) Eastern or Pacific oysters, drained and patted dry
¾ cup melted butter
1 tablespoon finely grated onion
½ teaspoon salt
about ¼ teaspoon freshly ground black pepper
¼ teaspoon dried thyme
3 cups fine soft bread crumbs (preferably sourdough French)
½ cup very finely chopped walnuts

Dip oysters in butter to coat and arrange in a single layer over bottom of a shallow casserole, about 1 quart. Sprinkle with onion, salt, pepper, and thyme. Toss bread crumbs with all but 2 tablespoons of the butter, and sprinkle over oysters. Bake in a moderate oven (350°) for 20 to 25 minutes or until crumbs are crisp and golden. Meantime, sauté walnuts in remaining 2 tablespoons butter until they toast lightly; turn over top of baked oysters. Makes 6 servings.

Wine suggestion: a Johannisberg Riesling, one of the California Chablis types, or a dry, tart rosé

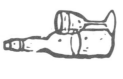

You hear about Clams and Rice and/or Cockles and Rice around San Francisco, and almost nowhere else along the Coast. Probably the local Italians invented it. You eat it with garlic-buttered, lightly toasted San Francisco sourdough bread. (San Francisco sourdough isn't the only answer to what bread to have with Western fish and shellfish, but it is one of the best. That really sour sourdough, chewy and crusty, particularly suits the straightforward fish dishes—grilled or broiled or fried fish, steamed clams, and the simple mayonnaise-dressed shellfish salads.)

CLAMS AND RICE, SAN FRANCISCO

3 pounds steaming clams
1 cup sliced green onions with part
   of green tops
1 large clove garlic, minced or mashed
½ cup chopped fresh parsley
¼ cup finely chopped green
   bell pepper
about 3 tablespoons olive oil
1 cup uncooked long-grain white rice
1 large ripe tomato,
   peeled and chopped
freshly ground black pepper
1½ cups water
additional chopped fresh parsley
lemon wedges

Scrub clams well with a brush; soak in cold water for 1 hour, drain, and rinse. In a large kettle, slowly sauté onions, garlic, parsley, and green pepper in olive oil until limp. Stir in rice, tomato, a generous grinding of black pepper, and water. Add clams. Cover and cook over medium heat for 20 minutes or until rice is tender. Taste broth and add salt if necessary. Serve in rimmed plates. Sprinkle with additional parsley; garnish with lemons. Makes 4 generous servings.

CRISP-FRIED SAND DABS WITH VINEGAR DIP

Sand dabs are the smallest of the West Coast flounders (called sole), and much appreciated around San Francisco and Monterey. They're best sautéed. Sometimes a recipe is best told by a fisherman's quotation:

"Clean (sand dabs). Don't bone. Salt and pepper and flour, and fry crisp in plenty of hot butter. Put hot crisp fish in a plate that has [in it] a mixture of vinegar (cider or wine, just to give tang), chopped parsley, and garlic cut in match-head-size chunks. Keep pouring hot crisp fried sand dabs into this plate and sauce as you eat 'em out."

Monterey Bay prawns are a delicacy —just around Monterey, and these just at irregular times. They are only in certain deep canyons along the Coast, and it is only at off times from salmon fishing that the fishermen can afford the time and tedium to seek them out. So they are usually a wintertime glory. You generally have to be a friend of a fisherman—and a very good friend— to know when he's caught some and to get a taste.

Monterey Bay prawns are sweet and marvelous whenever you can get them, but they're ethereal when they're with roe.

One preparation is to fry them in butter. You need nothing else if you go heavy on the butter. The butter has the salt. And you don't peel the prawns be-

forehand because you want to get all the prawn juices with the salty butter. You serve them heads on. To eat, break heads off; then eat all the sweet body meat. In butter-frying, the shells get crisp and crunchy, and you can eat shells and all. (You can do this same thing with other medium-size prawns; first cut down backs through shells and remove veins.)

BUTTER-SALTED MONTEREY BAY PRAWNS

Rinse and dry prawns. Heat a lot of butter in a frying pan just until it foams. Add prawns, and sauté over low heat just until pink and opaque. Serve with sautéeing butter as sauce. Grind on black pepper if you wish.

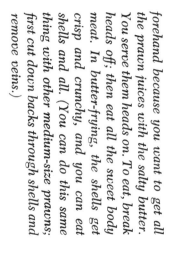

The fame of the Monterey Abalone Steak is unquestioned. Pop Ernst invented it, they say.

He discovered the way to trim (cut off dark portions) and steak (cut across grain into about three-eighth-inch-thick slices) and pound the meat to tenderness (with a wooden mallet, use light, rhythmical motions and pound each slice evenly until limp and velvety), and the secret of cooking (below). He invented that preparation over forty years ago and served it in his fish restaurant that stood at the Monterey end of the Monterey wharf. The old-timers remember Pop Ernst well, always standing out in front with his Shriner's fez on.

Nowadays, some cooks flour and egg and crumb abalone, but that's not Pop's way. All cooks agree that abalone has to be fast fried—flipped into the pan and on each side just to sizzle it. Otherwise, it will be tough. "You don't cook it; you just heat it through."

The browning butter is part of the taste.

POP ERNST'S ABALONE STEAKS

Wipe pounded steak with a damp cloth. Put into sizzling, very hot butter in a frying pan for 30 seconds on one side, 20 seconds on the other. Sprinkle with salt and pepper. Serve with lemon. That's all.

The Japanese were the first and are still the foremost abalone divers off Monterey and Morro Bay. (The season is mid-March to mid-January.) Ask them how to cook it, and they'll tell you, "Sashimi, not steak." Abalone sashimi is wonderfully fresh-tasting and crunchy.

At the beach, the Japanese just pry the meat out of the shell, rinse it, trim it, then score it, slice it, and "Dip it in soy and drink sake."

When serving abalone sashimi at home as hors d'oeuvres or a first course, you can make a more precise dipping sauce: Mix a little monosodium glutamate with Japanese soy sauce, and place in a small container. Mix wasabi powder (available in Japanese markets) with enough water to make a stiff paste; put into another small container. As you eat, mix wasabi with soy mixture according to your taste.

If you don't have an abalone diver among your friends, you can sometimes purchase live abalone in the shell in Japanese markets or from divers along the abalone coast.

ABALONE SASHIMI

Wash whole piece of meat from an abalone in cold water, and trim off all tough black edges. With a very sharp knife, score meat all across top and bottom surfaces about 1/8 inch apart and 1/4 inch deep. Slice meat across the scoring lines (right angles) into strips as thin as possible. Dip strips into soy or dipping sauce. Makes first course for about 6 people.

Among the dozen or so wholesale fish markets that stretch along the San Pedro (Terminal Island) wharf off Los Angeles, a few still run their business so that the fish unloading, cleaning, and sending out to markets takes place downstairs, and the office and a kitchen function upstairs. In those scrubbed little kitchens, some unbelievably good fish cooking takes place. The cooking in these places provides the midday meal for the fish-market workers, and the cooks use the choicest fresh fish that come in on the morning's boats.

In one of these upstairs kitchens, mild-mannered Frank Minighino presides. He selects and cooks all the fish.

His dishes seem to burst with the goodness of good fish, treated right and simply. On most days, he cooks three or four different fish dishes, except for the one day a week that is designated for pasta. At the stroke of noon each day, about twelve to fifteen workers settle around the big bare table; and Frank serves a feast of fishes, right out of their cooking pots—with Italian bread, oil-and-vinegar-dressed lettuce, and an easy-to-drink Italian red wine (hopefully one of the workers' homemade wines).

Modest Mr. Minighino says of his efforts, "It's all simple cooking. Whatever comes to my mind first, I cook."

Just our fellow workers eat here. Most of them are relations. They eat good. They got no squawk coming."

The fish workers say they eat "fisherman" style, and they know it's good, and they love it. They glory in the thought that their seafood is the only natural food left that has not been fed or treated artificially. (And they carry out this theme by drinking homemade wine.)

Totuava is the current Southern California splendor. It is caught from about December through May, a little south of San Diego, off Mexico; and it is locally credited to be the most refined of the white sea basses. The

elegant white meat is very sweet, flaky, and moist. It is a big fish, and an all-around fish to bake, broil, barbecue, and poach. It is usually filleted and the thick fillets cut into steaks.

Frank Minighino would choose the richest, tenderest piece of all, the tenderloin (belly or flank). He is just as likely to barbecue or broil it as to poach it, and he serves it with the lemon-oil sauce below.

(Incidentally, this same saucing is excellent on one-inch-thick steaks of Northwest sturgeon, barbecued.)

You can use this same treatment on a less regal sea bass.

POACHED TOTUAVA WITH LEMON-PEPPER OIL

3-pound totuava tenderloin
    or fillet piece
poaching liquid (recipe below)
½ cup *each* melted butter and
    olive oil
freshly ground black pepper
lemon wedges

Wipe fish with a damp cloth and wrap in cheesecloth. Lower fish into simmering poaching liquid, return to simmering, then cover and simmer until fish flakes, from 10 to 40 minutes depending on thickness of fillet. (If necessary, add water to make enough liquid to just cover fish in kettle.) Lift fish from liquid; drain well; unwrap, and turn onto warm serving plate. Combine butter and olive oil and heat to warm; pour half over fish; serve remaining half with fish. Garnish fish with lemon wedges. Let each guest grind on black pepper, squeeze on lemon juice, and add more butter-oil sauce to his taste. Makes 6 servings.

Poaching liquid: Combine the following ingredients in a kettle, cover, and simmer *for 20 minutes:* 1 quart water; 1 onion, sliced; 6 whole black peppercorns; 2 whole allspice; ½ cup dry white wine; 3 tablespoons lemon juice; 1 bay leaf; and 1 teaspoon salt.

CHAPTER 9

THE LEMON AFTER THE FISH
SWEET SUPPLEMENTS; THE LEMON FINISH

The love of lemon must be innate to seafood devotées. They seek that fresh lemon tartness again and again and never tire of it. No matter how much lemon is used to sauce and season a fish dish, they still crave more lemon after the fish; even a lemon dessert is not too much; it still seems the finest finish.

When our tastes demand that lemon for dessert after seafood, we may not know why, but the Western commercial citrus growers give a suggestion. They say that lemon juice will neutralize or keep the flesh of fish or shellfish from becoming alkaline, and that prevents the development of strong fishlike odors. Probably, then, lemon is good at the end of a meal simply because it so decisively ends the fishness of the meal.

Whether you choose it for a reason or simply on a whim, some form of lemon seems the only proper way to wind up a fish dinner—and that fact has led to this chapter.

This is a collection of some superb supplements to seafood eating. Admittedly it reflects a persuasion toward ginger as well as toward lemon.

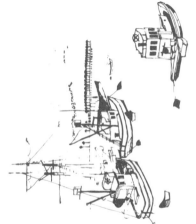

Garnish with fresh mint sprigs or lemon leaves.

LEMON-FROSTED FRESH PINEAPPLE

1 quart rich lemon ice cream
6 tablespoons finely chopped
   drained preserved ginger
fresh pineapple, cut
   into slender slices

Allow ice cream to soften slightly. Fold in ginger, then freeze until firm. Arrange pineapple slices slightly overlapping on dessert plates. Top with ice cream. Makes 6 servings.

LEMON PUDDING-CAKE AND CREAM

Good old-fashioned home cooks have been baking a form of this tart lemon pudding-cake for years, but not with the hot ginger and not with the cold whipped cream. The ginger is still optional.

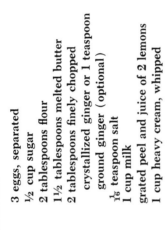

3 eggs, separated
½ cup sugar
2 tablespoons flour
1½ tablespoons melted butter
2 tablespoons finely chopped
   crystallized ginger or 1 teaspoon
   ground ginger (optional)
1/16 teaspoon salt
1 cup milk
grated peel and juice of 2 lemons
1 cup heavy cream, whipped

In a mixing bowl, beat egg yolks. Beat in sugar, then flour, butter, ginger, salt, milk, lemon peel, and lemon juice to make a smooth mixture. Separately beat egg whites until stiff but not dry, and fold into yolk mixture. Pour into a buttered baking dish (about 1½ quarts), set into a pan with hot water about 1 inch deep in bottom; bake in a slow oven (325°) for 55 minutes or until top is browned and knife inserted about halfway deep in center comes out clean. Spoon into serving dishes while warm. Top with whipped cream. Makes 5 to 6 servings.

The creamy richness of the sour cream makes the wood-fiberlike, crystalline structure of parfait only an appearance and not a taste-texture.

GINGER-LEMON PARFAIT WITH STRAWBERRIES

3 egg whites
⅛ teaspoon salt
1 cup brown sugar, firmly packed
1 cup water
2 teaspoons lemon juice
⅓ cup finely chopped
    crystallized or drained
    preserved ginger
2 tablespoons grated fresh lemon peel
2 cups commercial sour cream
sliced fresh strawberries

Beat egg whites with salt until stiff but not dry. Combine brown sugar and water in a saucepan, bring to a boil, then cook rapidly for 5 minutes without stirring. Pour hot syrup in a fine stream into egg whites, beating constantly. Continue beating until mixture is thick and cool. Stir in lemon juice, ginger, and lemon peel. Stir sour cream until smooth and fold in. Freeze until firm without stirring. Serve topped with sliced strawberries. Makes about 1¼ quarts or 8 servings.

PRINCE'S PUDDING

5 eggs
1¼ cups sugar
grated peel and juice of 1 lemon
lightly toasted sliced or slivered
  almonds (optional)

Beat eggs and sugar together until sugar is dissolved. Beat in lemon peel and juice. Pour into a shallow baking dish (3- to 4-cup size, so pudding is about 1 inch deep). Set into a pan with hot water ½ to 1 inch deep in bottom. Bake in a slow oven (325°) for 35 minutes or just until set. Remove from water; cool on a rack. Spoon into dessert dishes, and sprinkle lightly with almonds. Makes 5 servings.

Concentrated lemon and eggs, rather like a custard of all eggs and no milk. Spoon tiny portions into small dessert glasses, and top with toasted almonds.

A sheet of pastry separates the tart lemon filling into two levels. Chill the pie at least two hours, up to twelve hours before serving.

PASTRY LAYERED LEMON PIE

lemon filling (recipe below)	2 tablespoons sugar
pastry (below)	1 teaspoon vanilla
1 cup heavy (whipping) cream	grated semi-sweet chocolate

Turn half the cooled lemon filling into baked pie shell. Top with pastry circle (if it breaks, simply replace in shape). Top with remaining lemon filling. Beat cream with sugar and vanilla until whipped; spread over top of pie. Sprinkle lightly with grated chocolate. Chill. Makes 8 servings.

Lemon filling: Mix together in top part of double boiler 6 tablespoons cornstarch (measured level but packed), 2 cups sugar, ⅜ teaspoon salt, grated peel of 3 large lemons, and ⅔ cup fresh lemon juice. Beat 6 egg yolks and add; beat mixture until smooth. Gradually add 2 cups boiling water, stirring briskly. Place over hot water and cook, stirring, until thickened and smooth. Add 3 tablespoons butter. Allow to cool, stirring occasionally.

Pastry: Sift 1½ cups flour and ¾ teaspoon salt together into mixing bowl. With pastry blender, cut in ½ cup lard until particles are the size of small peas. Add just enough cold water to moisten particles (about 3 tablespoons), tossing with a fork to mix. Gather into a ball. On a lightly floured board, roll out two thirds of the dough into a circle to line a 9-inch pie pan; place in pan, forming a high fluted edge; prick well with a floured fork. Roll out remaining dough into a circle about 8 inches in diameter; place on baking sheet; prick with a fork. Bake in a hot oven (425°) until golden brown, about 7 minutes for circle, 10 minutes for shell. Cool on a rack.

LAVISH LEMON BUTTER

6 tablespoons butter
grated peel of 1 lemon
⅓ cup lemon juice
1 cup sugar
⅛ teaspoon salt
2 whole eggs
2 egg yolks

Melt butter in top of double boiler. Stir in lemon peel, lemon juice, sugar, and salt. Slightly beat whole eggs with egg yolks and stir into butter mixture. Cook over boiling water, beating constantly with a wire whisk, until thick and smooth, about 15 minutes. Cool. Makes about 1½ cups.

Note: You can store lemon butter, covered, in refrigerator for 4 weeks or more.

This cheese dessert depends on the lemon of a lovely lemon butter.

Arrange on a tray a brick of room-temperature cream cheese, a pot of lemon butter, red currant jelly, a basket of flaky butter puff wafers, and knives for spreading. Spread layers of cheese, lemon butter, and jelly on top of wafers. A tawny port complements.

The voluptuousness of that lemon butter is so satisfying by itself it seems it couldn't be put into another position without some loss. But it becomes the most compelling counterpoise to rich vanilla ice cream when the two are ribbon-layered together between a flaky pie crust and a toasted meringue.

LEMON LAYERED MERINGUE PIE

1 quart rich vanilla ice cream
9-inch baked pie shell
lemon butter (recipe opposite page)
3 egg whites
¼ teaspoon cream of tartar
few grains of salt
6 tablespoons sugar

Press layer scoops of half the ice cream firmly over bottom of cooled pie shell; freeze firm. Spread half the cooled lemon butter over ice-cream layer; freeze firm. Cover with a layer of remaining ice cream, and freeze firm. Top with remaining lemon butter, and freeze firm. Beat egg whites with cream of tartar and salt until foamy. Gradually beat in sugar, adding it a little at a time. Continue beating until sugar is dissolved and whites are stiff and glossy. Spread over top of pie, sealing well at edge of crust. Place pie on a board. Bake in a very hot oven (475°) until meringue is lightly browned, about 3 to 5 minutes. Serve immediately. Or freeze (remove pie from freezer 5 minutes before serving). Makes 6 to 8 servings.

COOL LEMON RICOTTA

1 pound fresh ricotta cheese
about 4 teaspoons superfine
  granulated sugar
3 tablespoons Strega liqueur
2 teaspoons grated fresh lemon peel
4 thin slices lemon

Beat ricotta with a fork until soft. Stir in sugar, Strega, and lemon peel. Spoon into 4 sherbet glasses. Chill thoroughly. Garnish each serving with a lemon slice. Makes 4 servings.

From a San Franciscan of Neapolitan descent.

This is one time to except the idea of room-temperature cheese; this should be a soothing cold cheese.

Fill and finish this within a few hours of serving time if possible. In a moment of poverty, the crust can work without the nuts.

LEMON MACADAMIA TART

1 cup unsifted all-purpose flour
3 tablespoons powdered sugar
½ cup butter
½ cup finely chopped salted
    macadamia nuts
key lemon custard (recipe below)
meringue (below)

Sift flour and sugar into mixing bowl. Cut in butter until particles are fine. Stir in macadamia nuts. Chill for 30 minutes. Turn into a 9-inch pie pan or French tart pan. Press into bottom and sides to form a crust. Bake in a hot oven (425°) for 8 to 12 minutes, until lightly browned. Cool on a rack. Turn key lemon custard into cooled shell. Spread meringue over filling, sealing well at edge of crust. Bake in a hot oven (400°) for 8 to 10 minutes or until delicately browned. Makes 6 servings.

Key lemon custard: Beat together until smooth and thickened, with rotary or electric beater, 3 egg yolks, 1 can (15 ounces) sweetened condensed milk, 1 teaspoon grated fresh lemon peel, and ½ cup fresh lemon juice.

Meringue: Beat 3 egg whites with ¼ teaspoon cream of tartar and a few grains of salt until foamy. Gradually beat in 6 tablespoons sugar, adding it about a tablespoon at a time. Continue beating until sugar is dissolved and whites are stiff and glossy.

GINGER APRICOTS

1 cup (6 ounces) moist dried
   apricot halves
1 teaspoon grated fresh lemon peel
about 2 cups cold water
¼ cup moist golden raisins
½ cup brown sugar, firmly packed
¼ teaspoon ground ginger

Place apricots in a saucepan with lemon peel and water to cover. Bring to a boil; reduce heat, and simmer for 20 minutes or until apricots are tender. Add raisins, brown sugar, and ginger, and simmer for 5 minutes more. Allow fruits to cool in syrup. Serve warm or chilled. Makes about 4 servings.

Serve this alone as a compote (perhaps with cream) or on top of lemon ice cream.

Lemon sherbet could hardly be simpler or more refreshing than this. Bake gingersnaps to go with it.

LEMON CREAM SHERBET

2 eggs
½ cup sugar
½ cup light corn syrup
2 cups half and half (half milk and
  half cream)
2 teaspoons grated lemon peel
¼ cup fresh lemon juice

Beat eggs and sugar together until thick and light colored. Stir in syrup, half and half, lemon peel, and juice. Freeze until almost firm. Beat until smooth, return to freezer, and freeze firm (or beat once more before freezing firm). Makes about 1 quart or 6 servings.

LEMON-CRESTED CHEESECAKE

1 box (6 ounces) zwieback, crushed to fine crumbs (1½ cups crumbs)
3 tablespoons sugar
6 tablespoons melted butter
3 large packages (8 ounces *each*) softened cream cheese
1 tablespoon vanilla
½ teaspoon salt
4 large eggs
1 cup sugar
lemon topping (recipe below)

Mix crumbs, the 3 tablespoons sugar, and butter, and press over bottom and sides of a buttered 9-inch spring-form pan. In a large mixing bowl, beat cheese with vanilla and salt until smooth and fluffy. Separately, with clean beaters, beat eggs with the 1 cup sugar until thick and light colored; gradually add to cheese mixture and beat until smooth. Turn into crumb-lined pan. Bake in a moderate oven (350°) for about 30 minutes. Cool on a rack. When thoroughly cool, spread with lemon topping. Cover and chill. Remove sides from pan and cut into wedges. Makes 12 servings.

Lemon topping: In a saucepan, mix together ⅔ cup sugar, 3 tablespoons cornstarch, and ¼ teaspoon salt. Add ¾ cup boiling water, and cook mixture over medium heat, stirring, until thick and smooth, about 4 minutes. Beat 1 egg, beat or whisk in a little of the hot mixture, then whisk back into thickened mixture along with 1 tablespoon butter. Cook for 2 minutes more, stirring with a whisk. Remove from heat, and stir in 1 teaspoon grated fresh lemon peel, 3 tablespoons fresh lemon juice, and 1 teaspoon vanilla. Cool thoroughly.

For fullest flavor, return almost to room temperature before serving.

What the Genoese conceive and cook in the way of fish demands a Genoese finish. A lemony Zabaglione is that. Here, light rum substitutes for the usual Marsala, and makes a lighter, drier, and more spirited Zabaglione.

Sprinkle lightly with semi-sweet chocolate curls, if you wish.

153

LEMON RUM ZABAGLIONE

6 egg yolks
6 tablespoons sugar
½ teaspoon grated lemon peel
6 tablespoons light dry rum

Beat egg yolks, sugar, and lemon peel together in top of double boiler. Place over hot (not boiling) water and gradually beat in rum. Cook, beating constantly with a wire whip or rotary beater, until thick, light, and smooth, about 5 to 10 minutes. Pour into small, stemmed glasses and serve immediately, or chill. Makes 4 servings.

LEMON FRESH PINEAPPLE PIE

Lemon somehow mellows the pineapple's sweet sharpness.

2 eggs
1½ cups sugar
2 tablespoons flour
1½ tablespoons grated
   fresh lemon peel
1 tablespoon fresh lemon juice
⅛ teaspoon salt
about 3 cups bite-size chunks of
   fresh pineapple (fruit from about
   1 medium-size pineapple)
pastry for double or lattice-crust
   9-inch pie
   sugar

Beat eggs slightly and beat in sugar, flour, lemon peel, lemon juice, and salt. Fold in pineapple. Line pie pan with half the pastry. Turn in pineapple mixture. Cover pie with top crust, cut with a decorative vent (or a lattice top). Flute edges to seal. Sprinkle very lightly with sugar. Bake in a hot oven (425°) for 40 to 45 minutes or until crust is brown. Cool. Makes 6 servings.

Good as it is warm and fresh, this is one cake that should really be baked a day or even two days before eating. With some aging, the lemon flavor comes up; without aging, the lemon is too soft.

A lemony butter cake makes the cake base and pushes up among the apples as it bakes. Melted butter, lemon peel, and sugar glaze the baking apple slices.

Top cake servings with whipped cream lightly sweetened with sugar, flavored with vanilla, and very lightly dusted with cinnamon.

LEMONY APPLE CAKE

½ cup soft butter
½ cup sugar
2 eggs
grated peel of 2 lemons
2 tablespoons fresh lemon juice
⅛ teaspoon salt
1 cup sifted all-purpose flour
5 tart cooking apples, peeled and cut into ⅛-inch-thick lengthwise slices
3 tablespoons melted butter
about 6 tablespoons sugar

Cream together butter and sugar thoroughly. Add eggs one at a time, and beat in thoroughly. Beat in grated peel of 1 lemon, 1 teaspoon of the lemon juice, and salt. Gradually add flour, and beat until mixture is smooth. Turn batter into buttered 9-inch spring-form pan or cake pan with removable bottom. Toss apple slices with the remaining lemon juice, and arrange evenly over batter. Mix melted butter and remaining lemon peel, and spoon evenly over apples; sprinkle with the 6 tablespoons sugar. Bake in a moderate oven (350°) for 1 hour or until apples are golden brown. Cool in pan on a rack. Makes 8 servings.

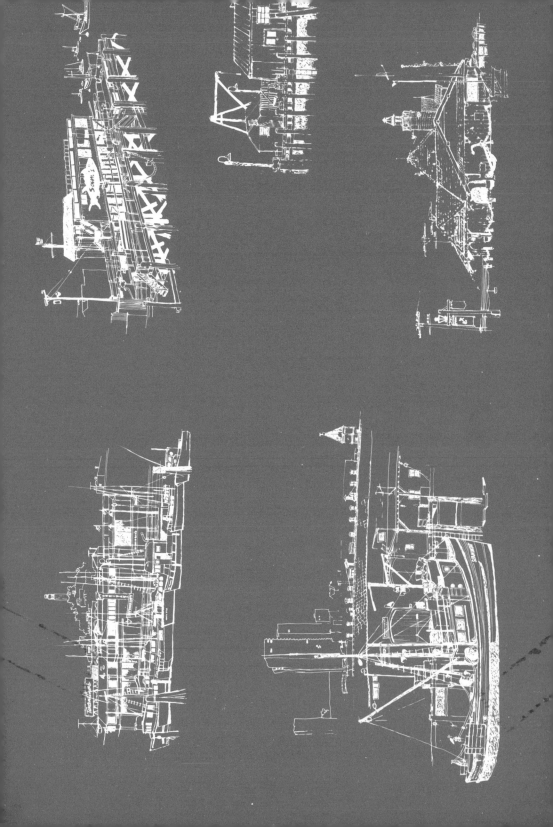